The Queer Heroes Coloring Book

Edited by the tag-team of terror
Jon Macy and Tara Madison Avery

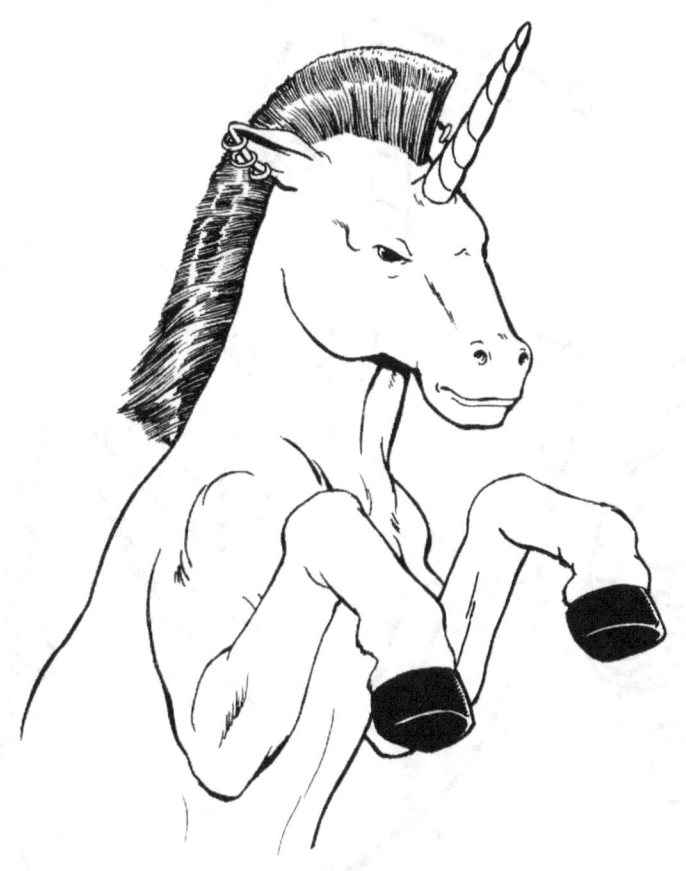

Stacked Deck Press

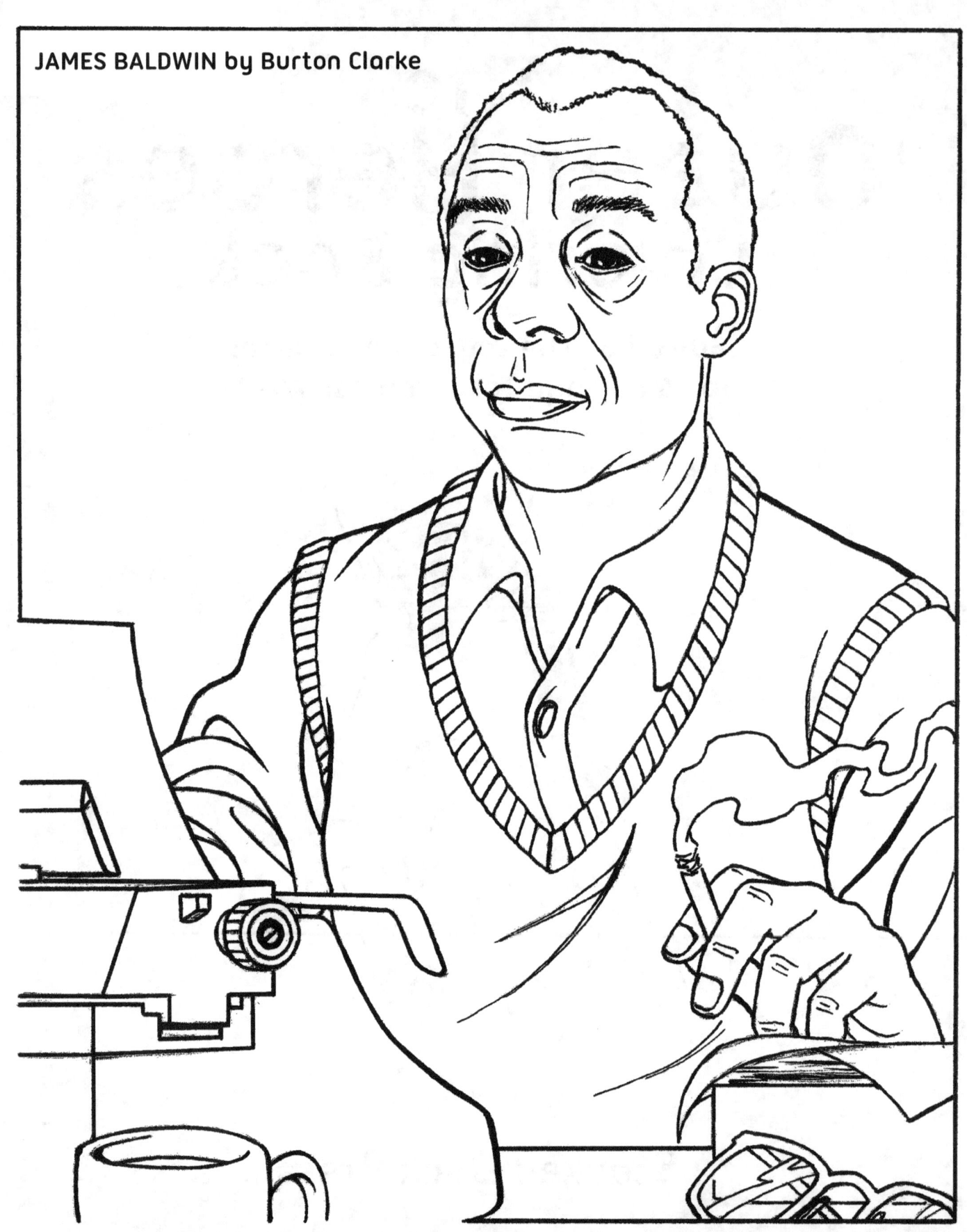

JAMES BALDWIN by Burton Clarke

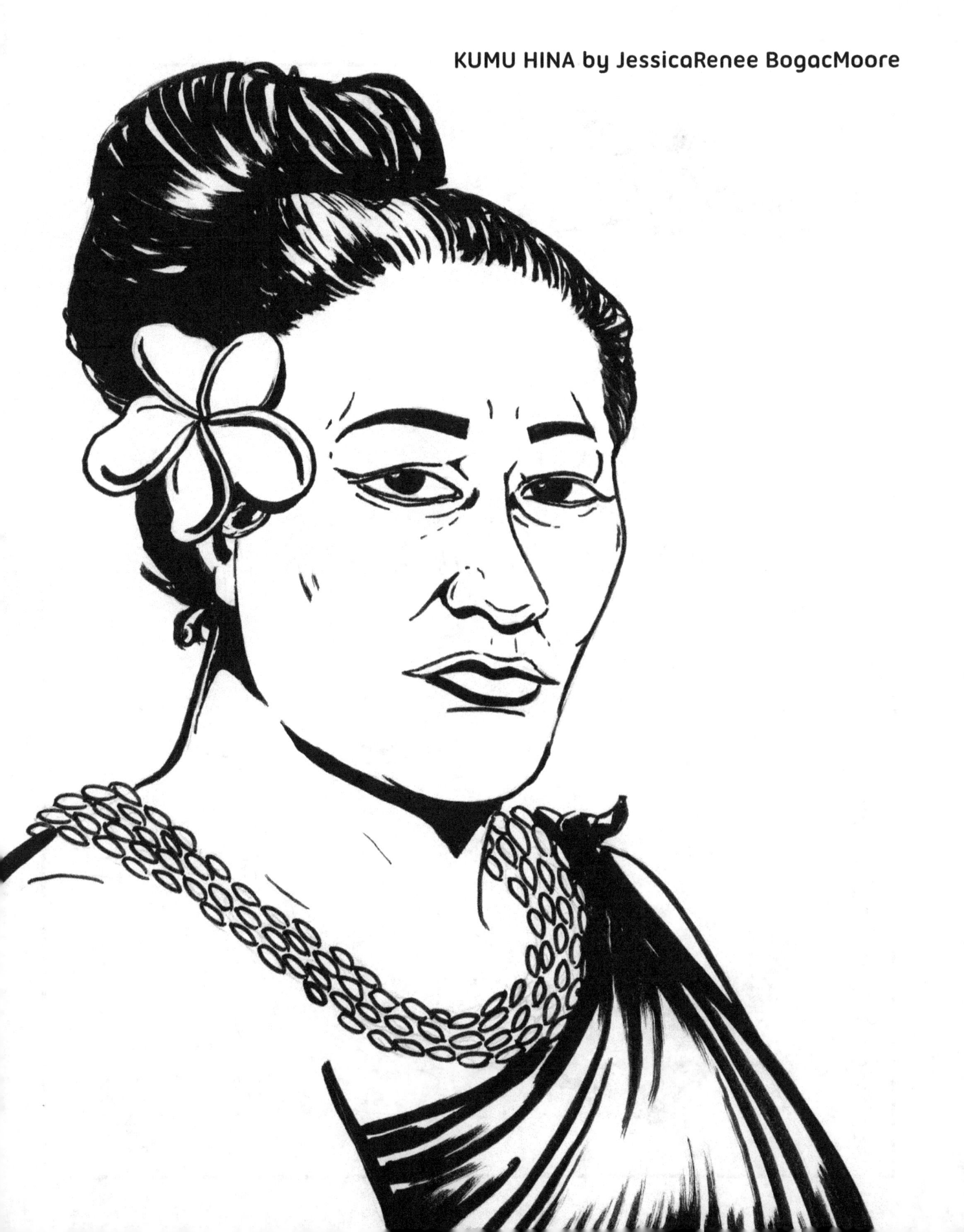

KUMU HINA by JessicaRenee BogacMoore

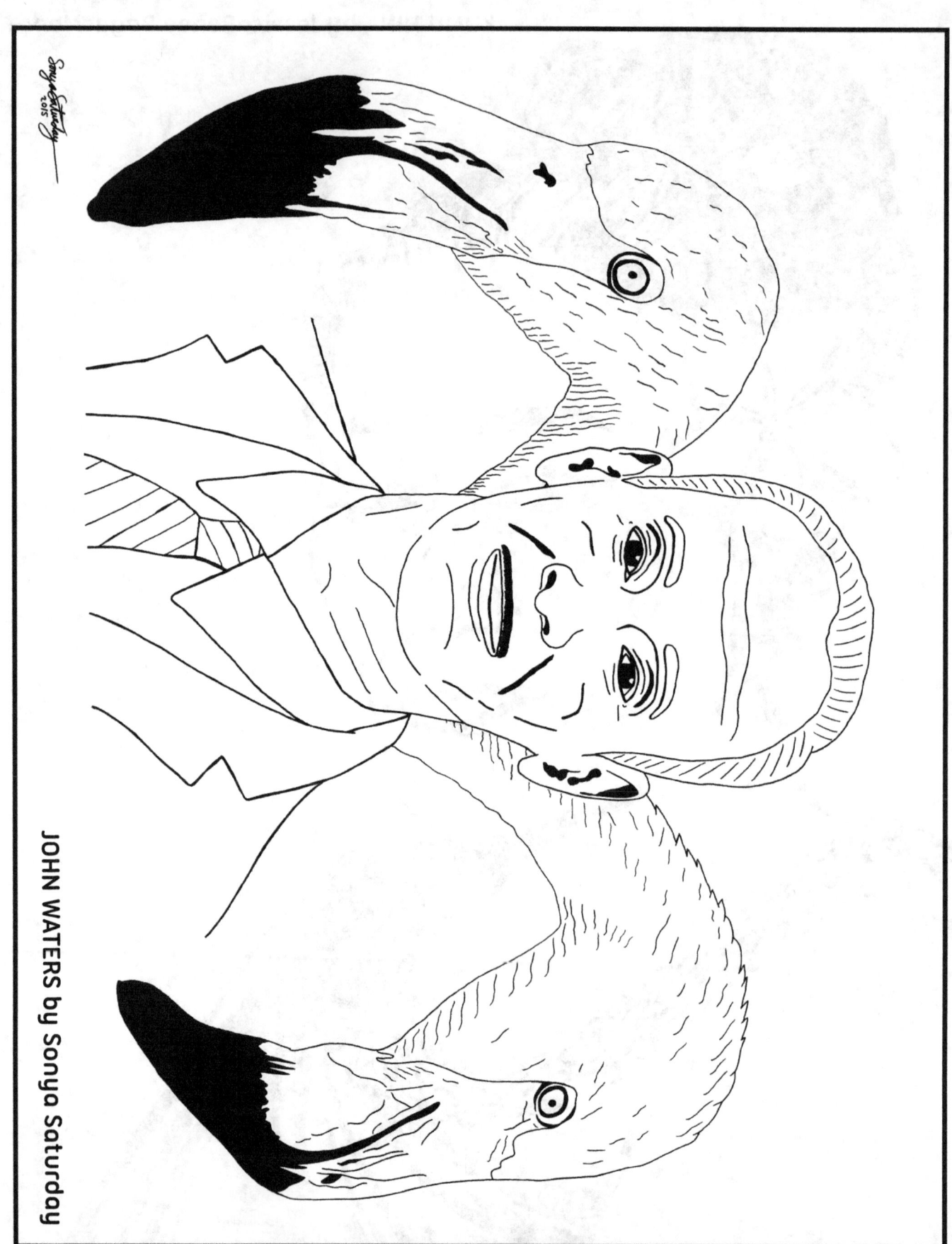

JOHN WATERS by Sonya Saturday

"I, MABEL HAMPTON, HAVE BEEN A LESBIAN ALL MY LIFE ... AND I AM PROUD OF MYSELF AND MY PEOPLE ... MY GAY PEOPLE AND MY BLACK PEOPLE."

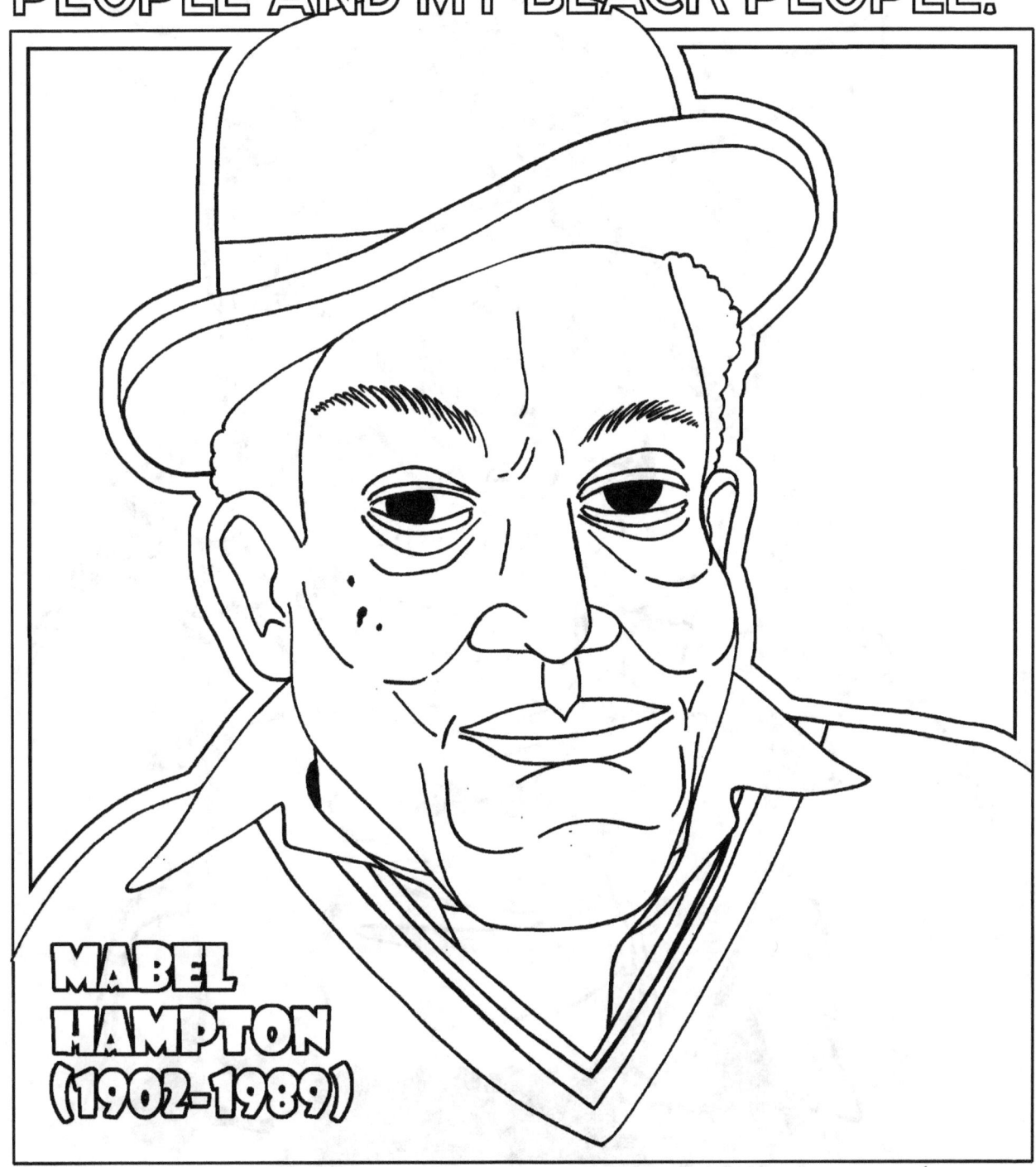

MABEL HAMPTON (1902-1989)

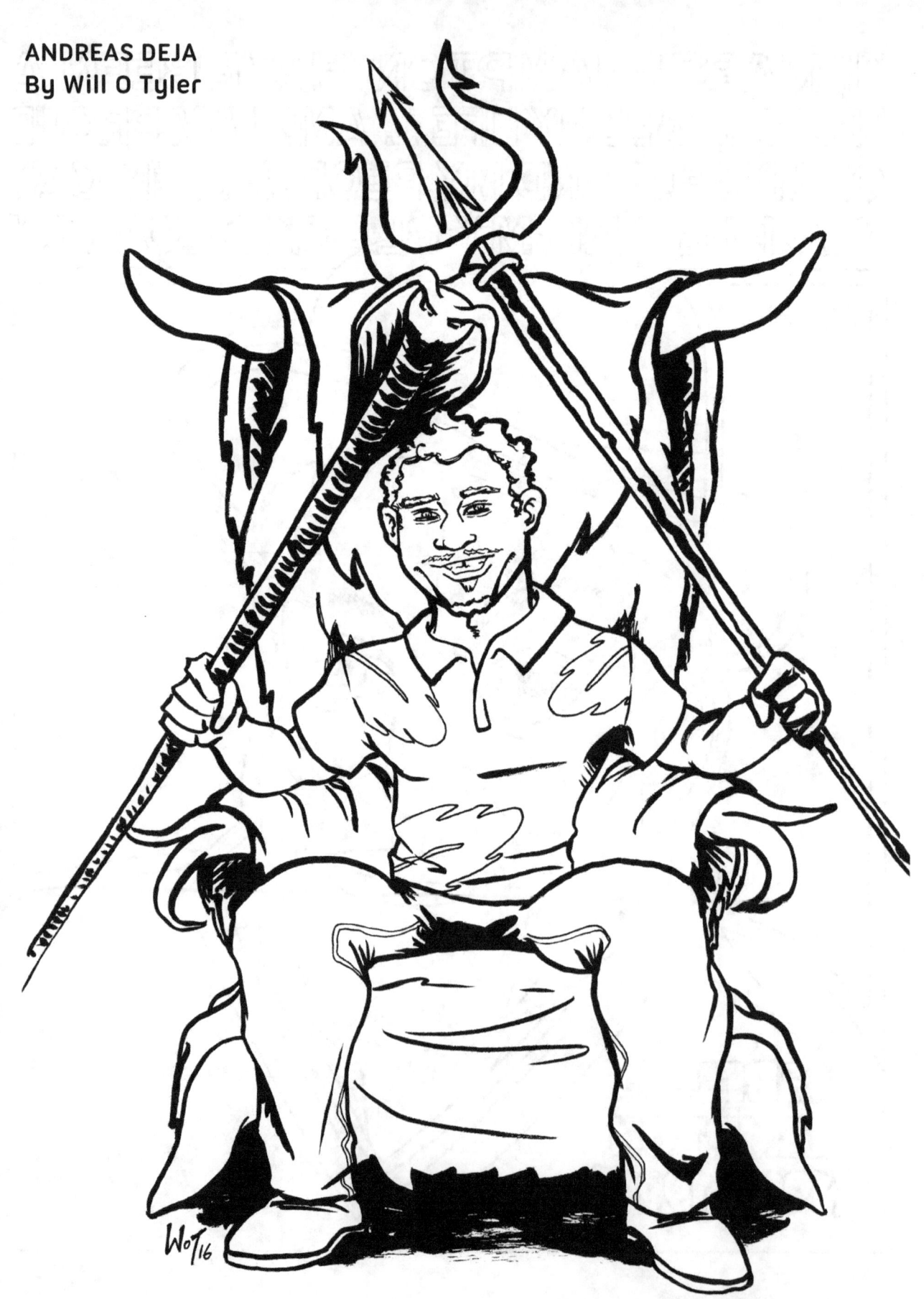

ANDREAS DEJA
By Will O Tyler

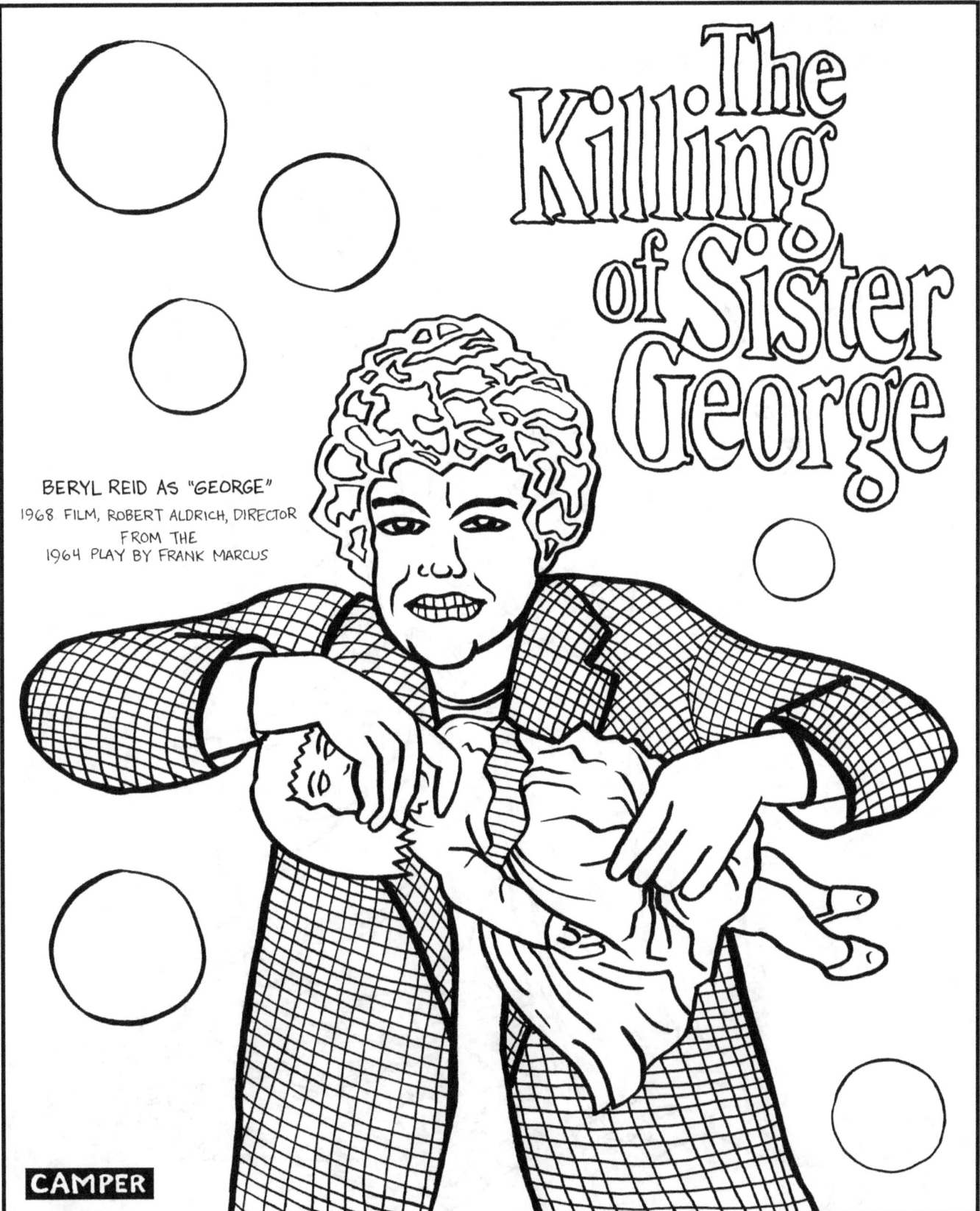

The Killing of Sister George

BERYL REID AS "GEORGE"
1968 FILM, ROBERT ALDRICH, DIRECTOR
FROM THE
1964 PLAY BY FRANK MARCUS

CAMPER

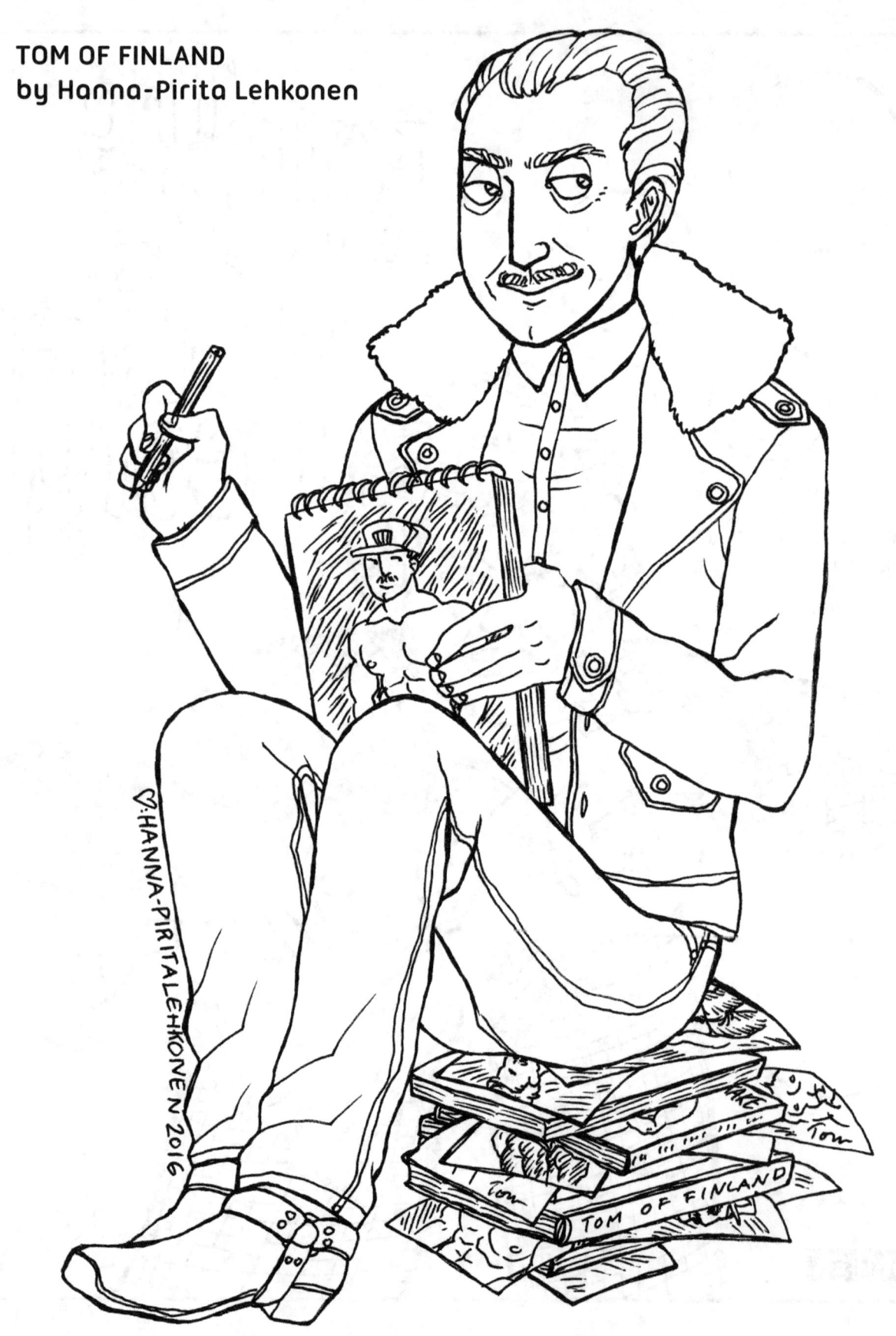

TOM OF FINLAND
by Hanna-Pirita Lehkonen

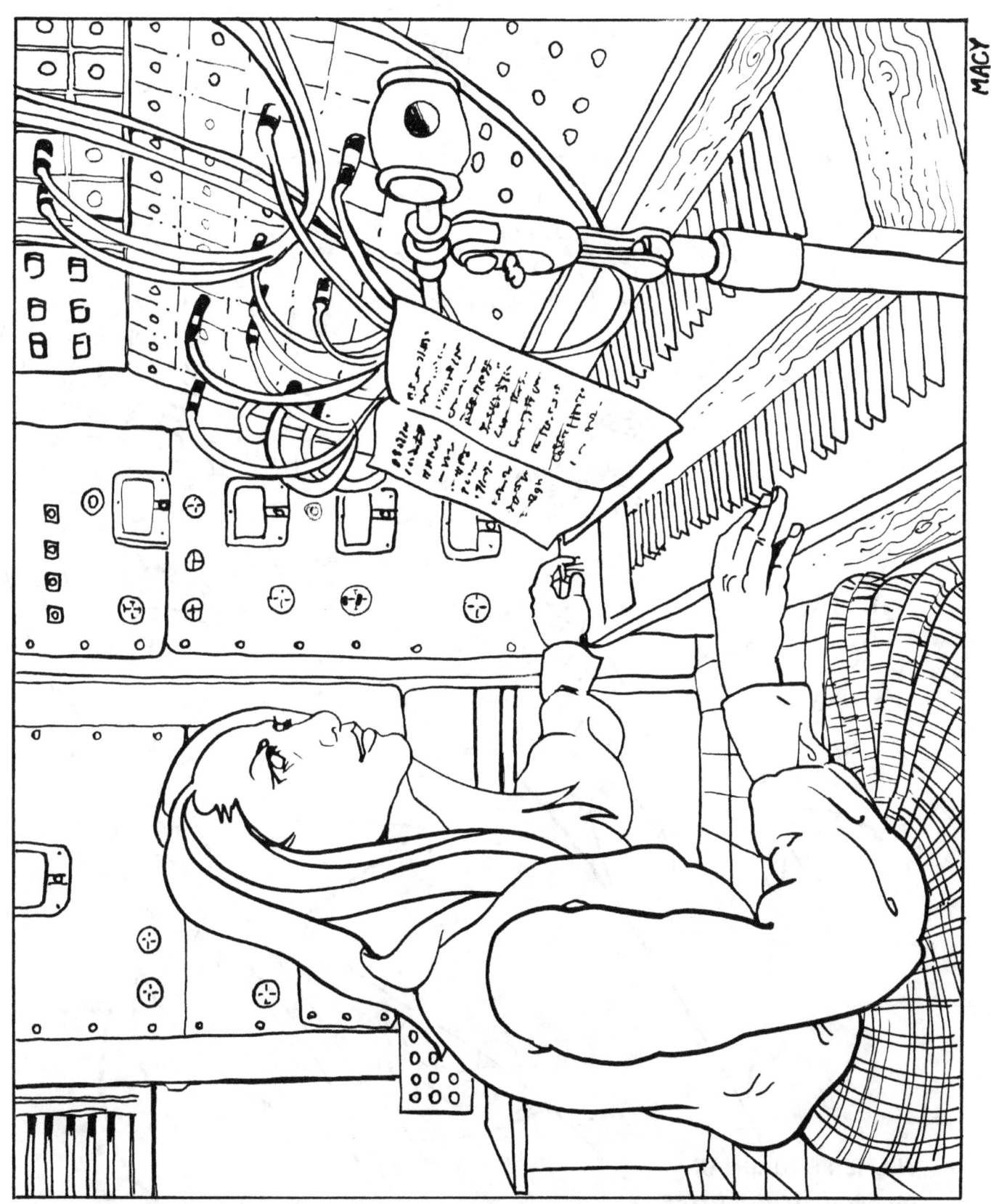

WENDY CARLOS by Jon Macy

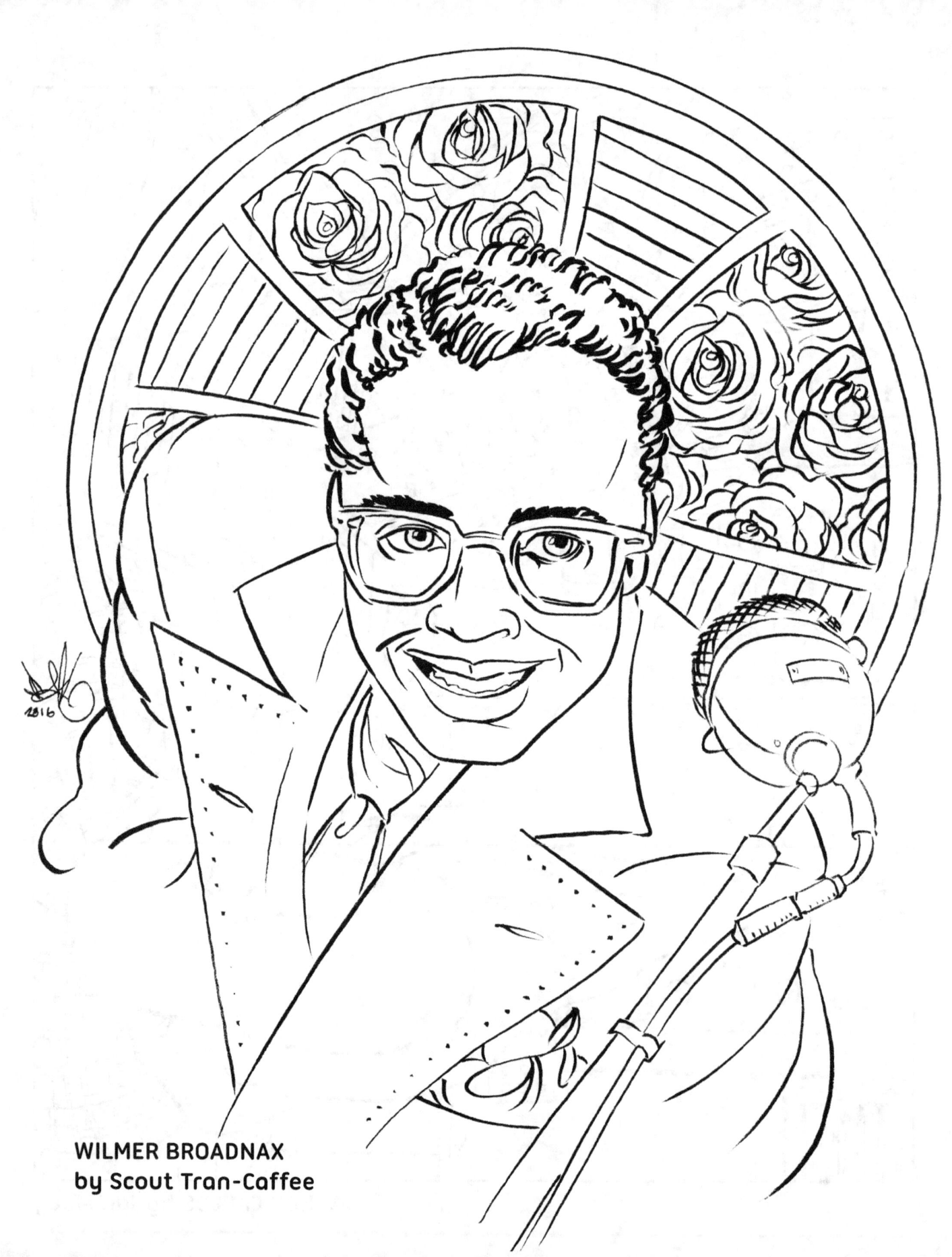

WILMER BROADNAX
by Scout Tran-Caffee

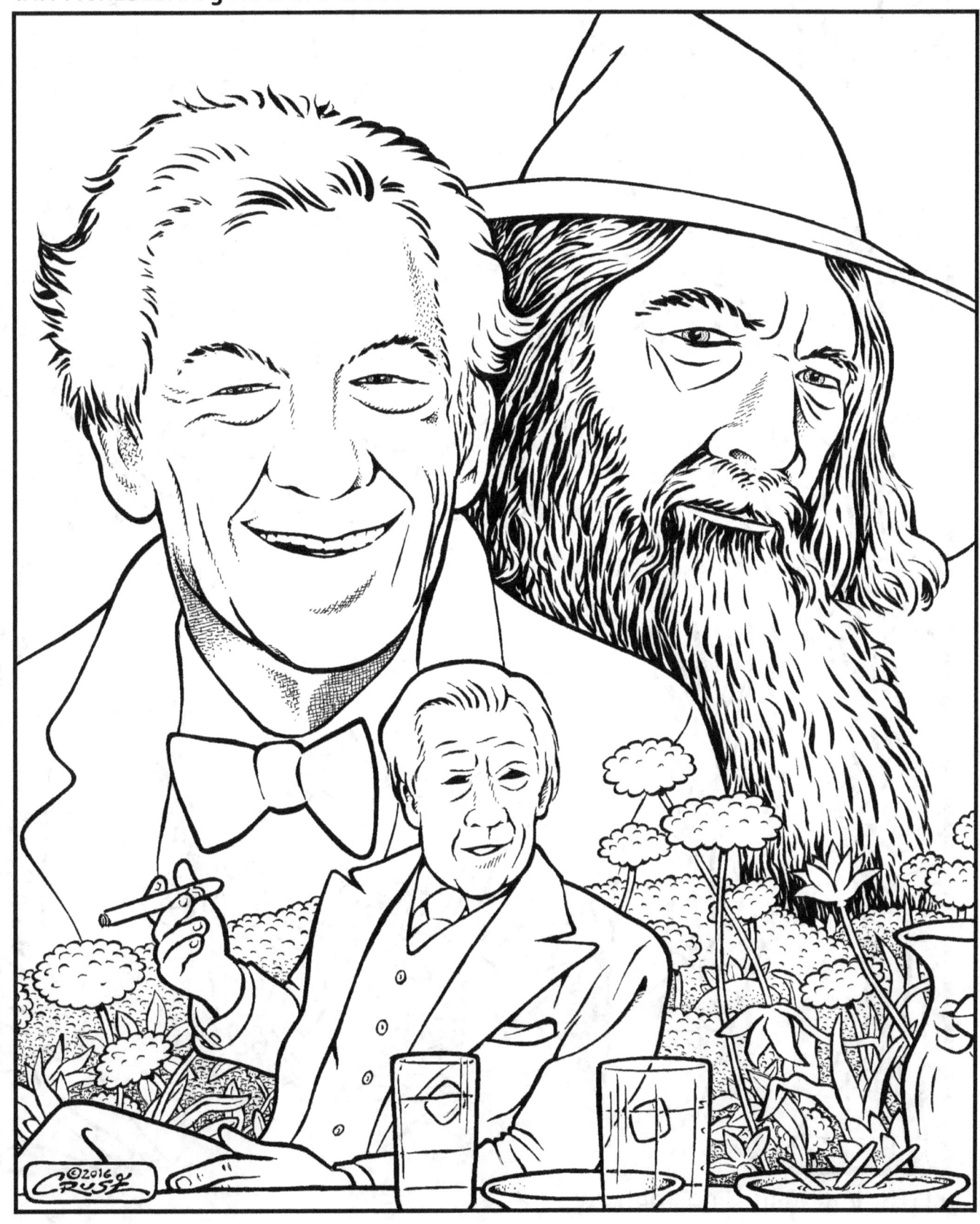

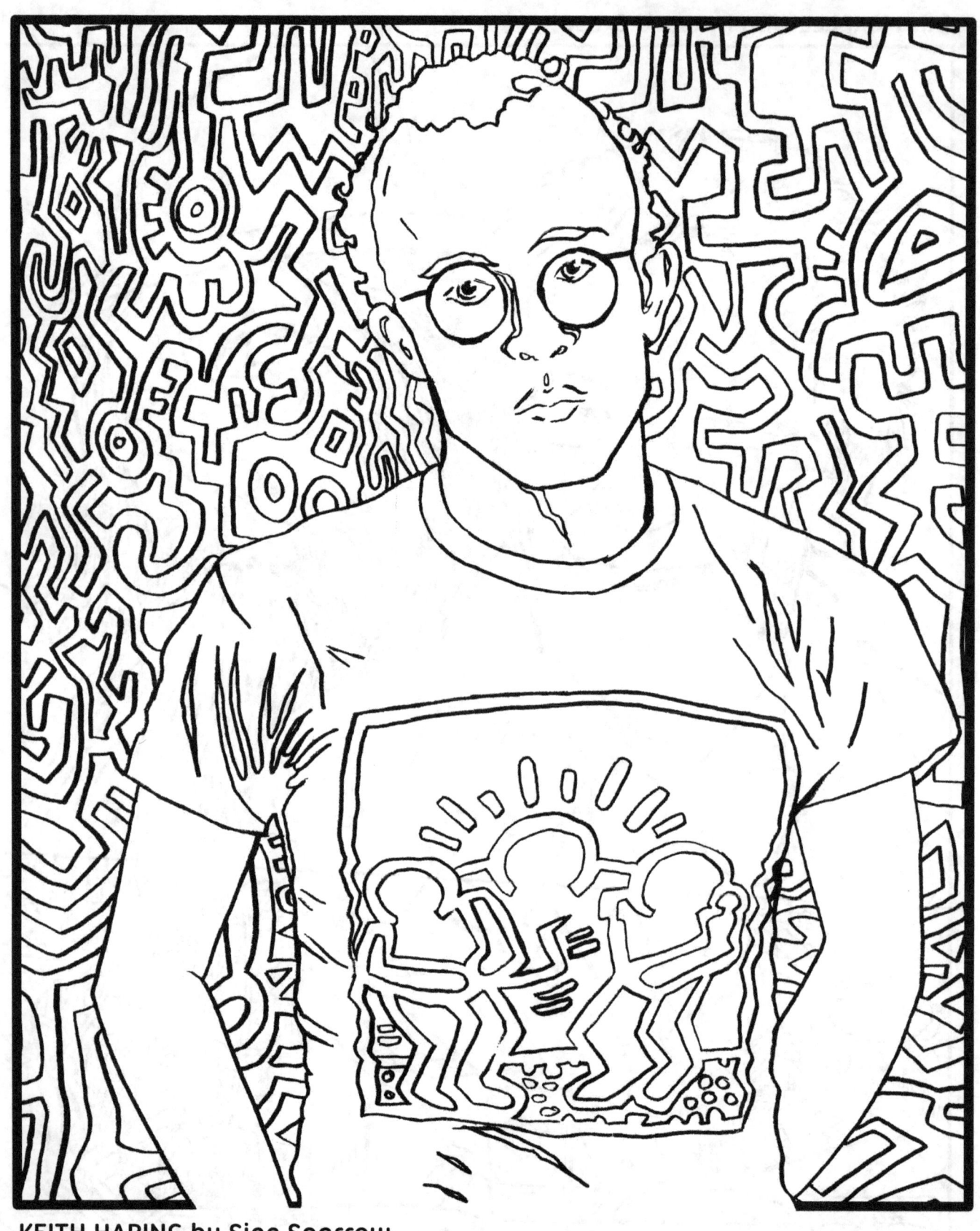

KEITH HARING by Sina Sparrow

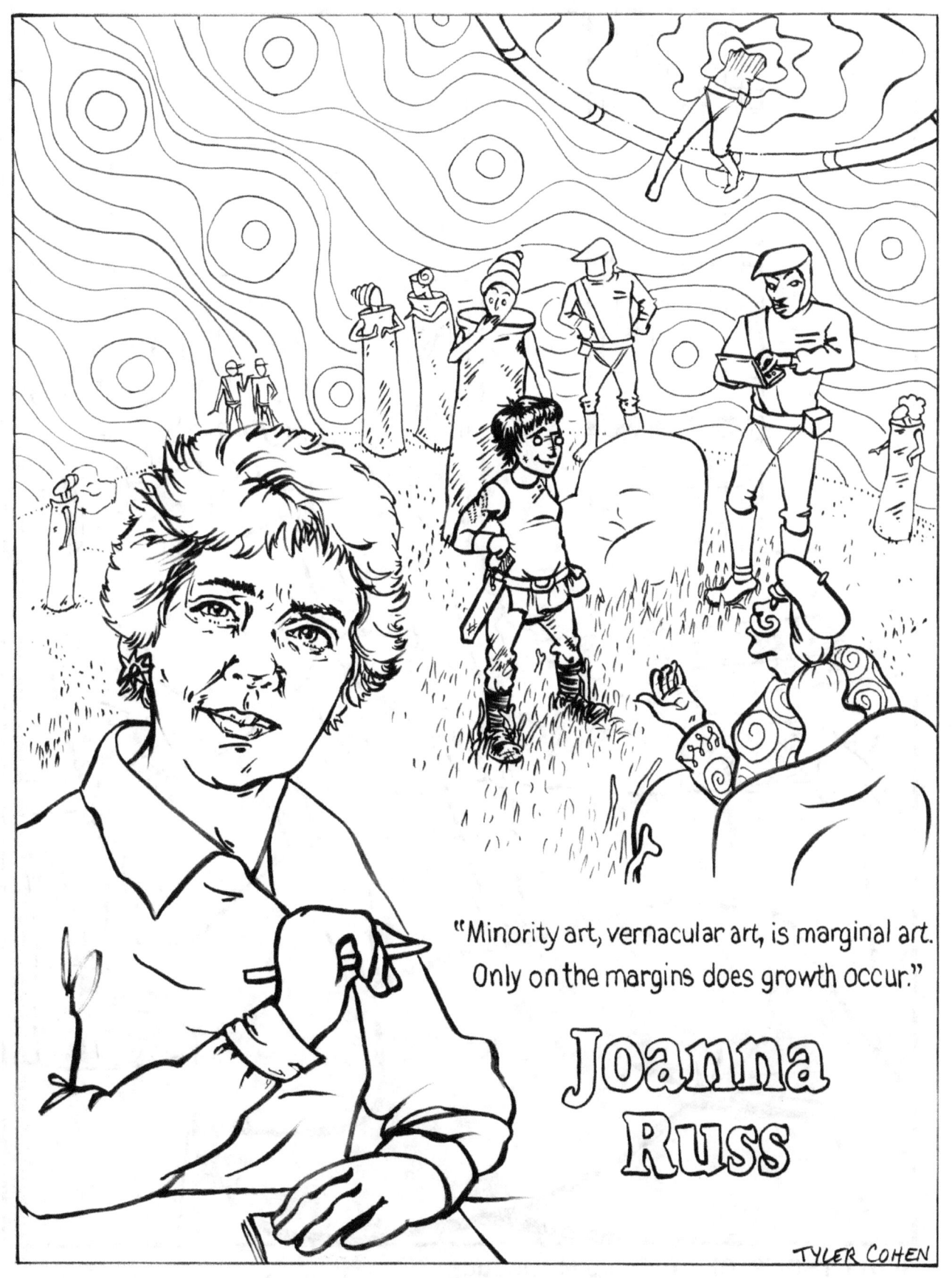

"Minority art, vernacular art, is marginal art. Only on the margins does growth occur."

Joanna Russ

TYLER COHEN

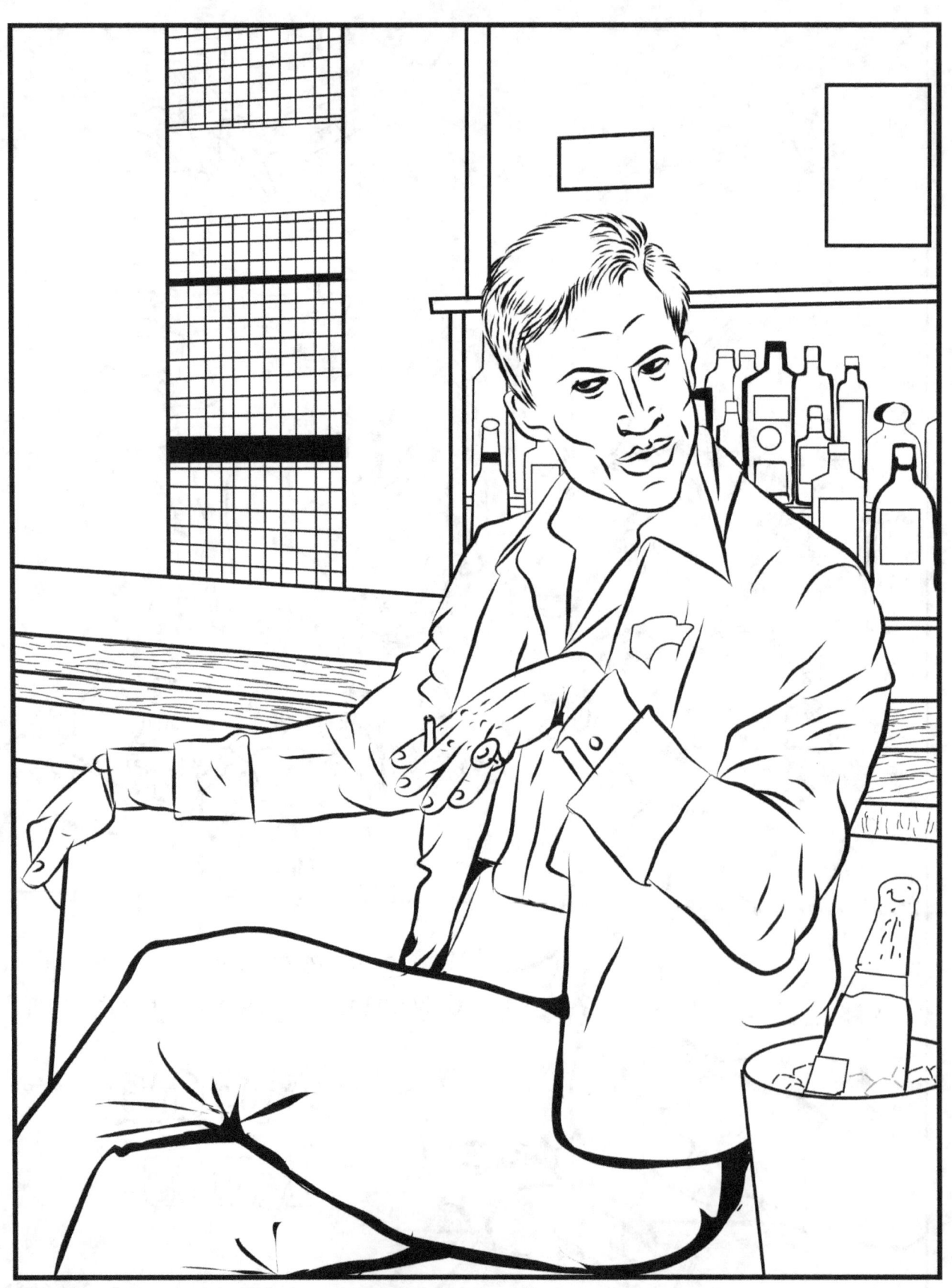

SCOTT THOMPSON by Steve MacIsaac

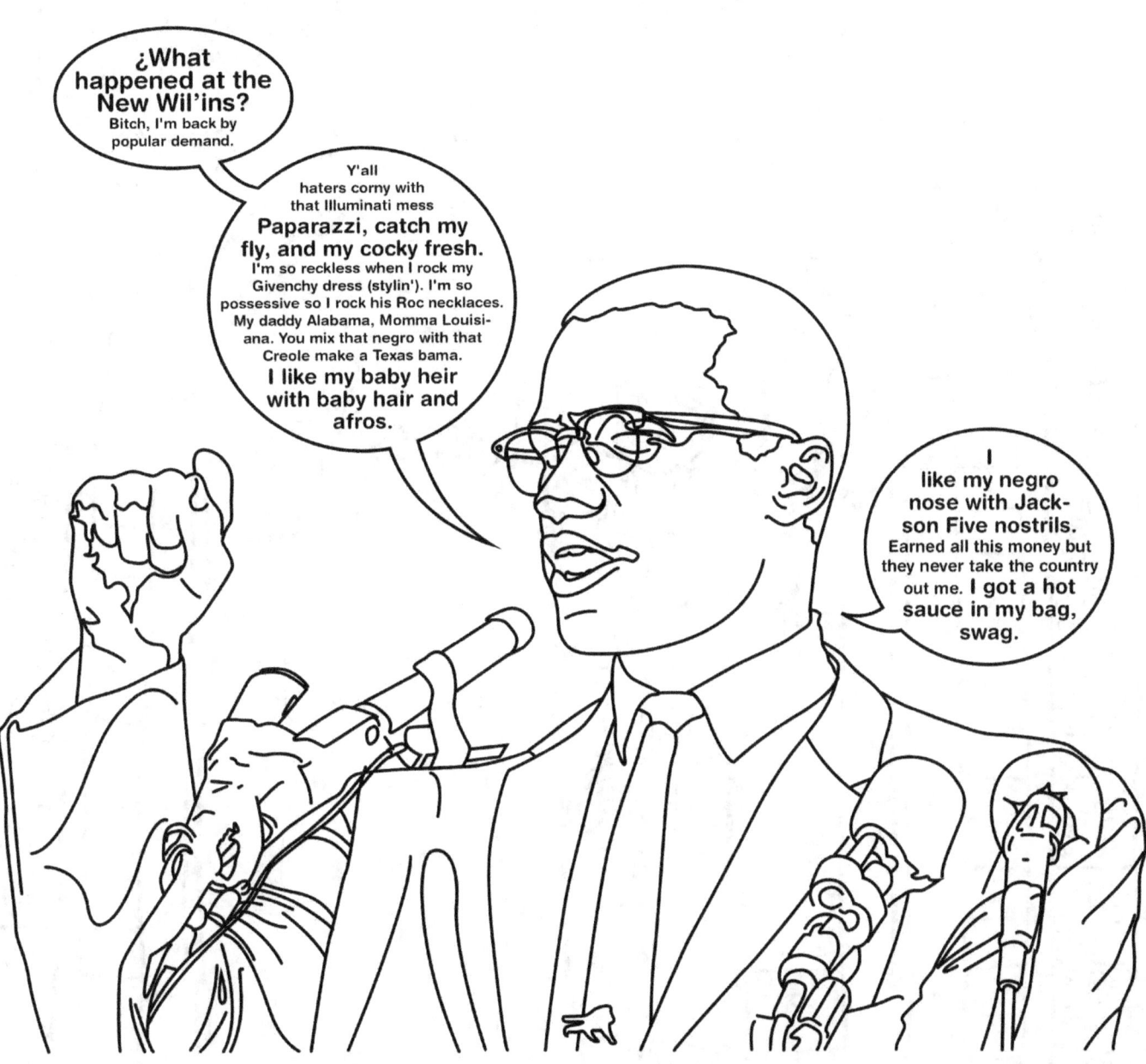

MALCOLM X
by Diego Gomez

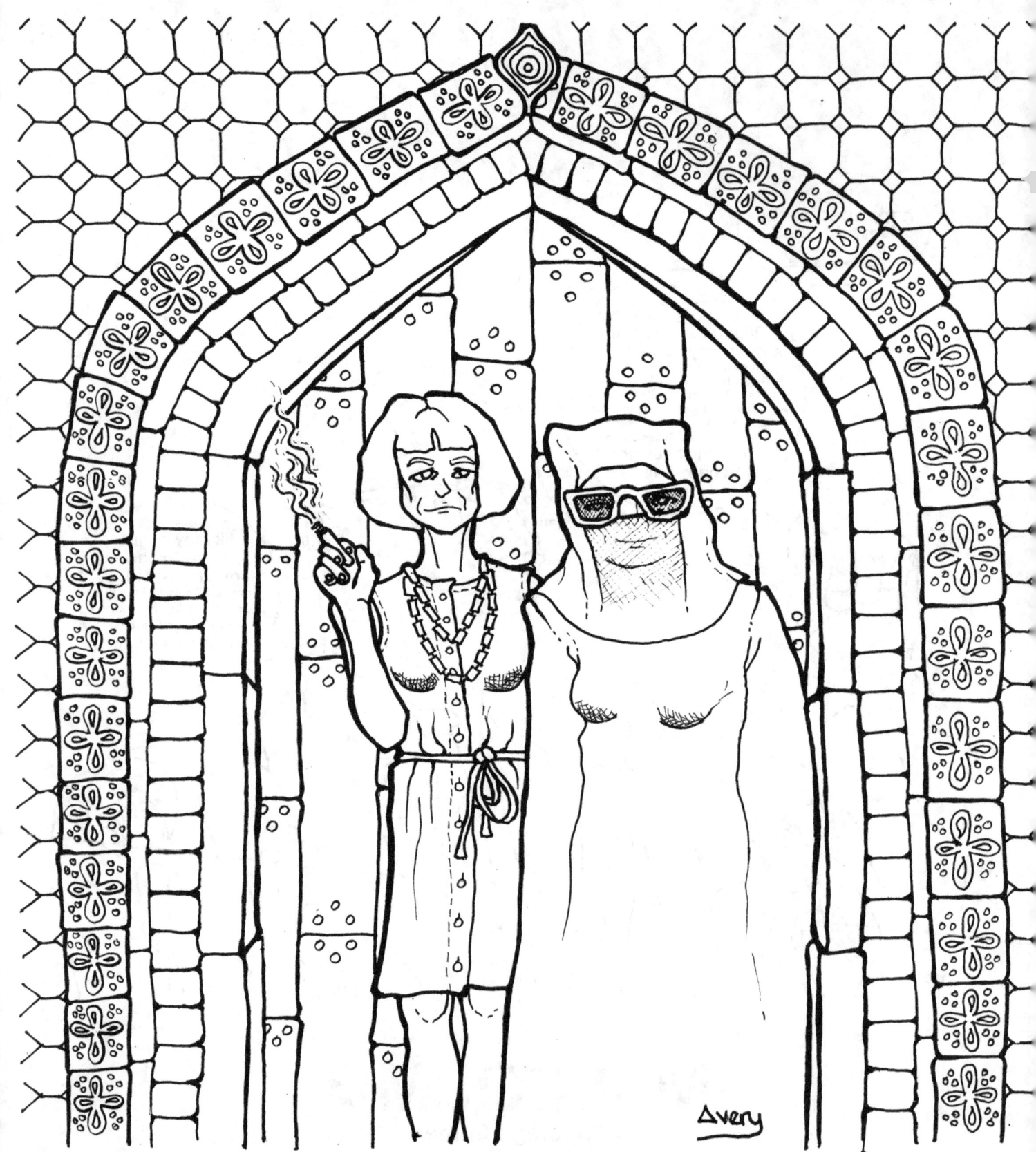

JANE BOWLES AND HER LOVER CHERIFA by Avery Cassell

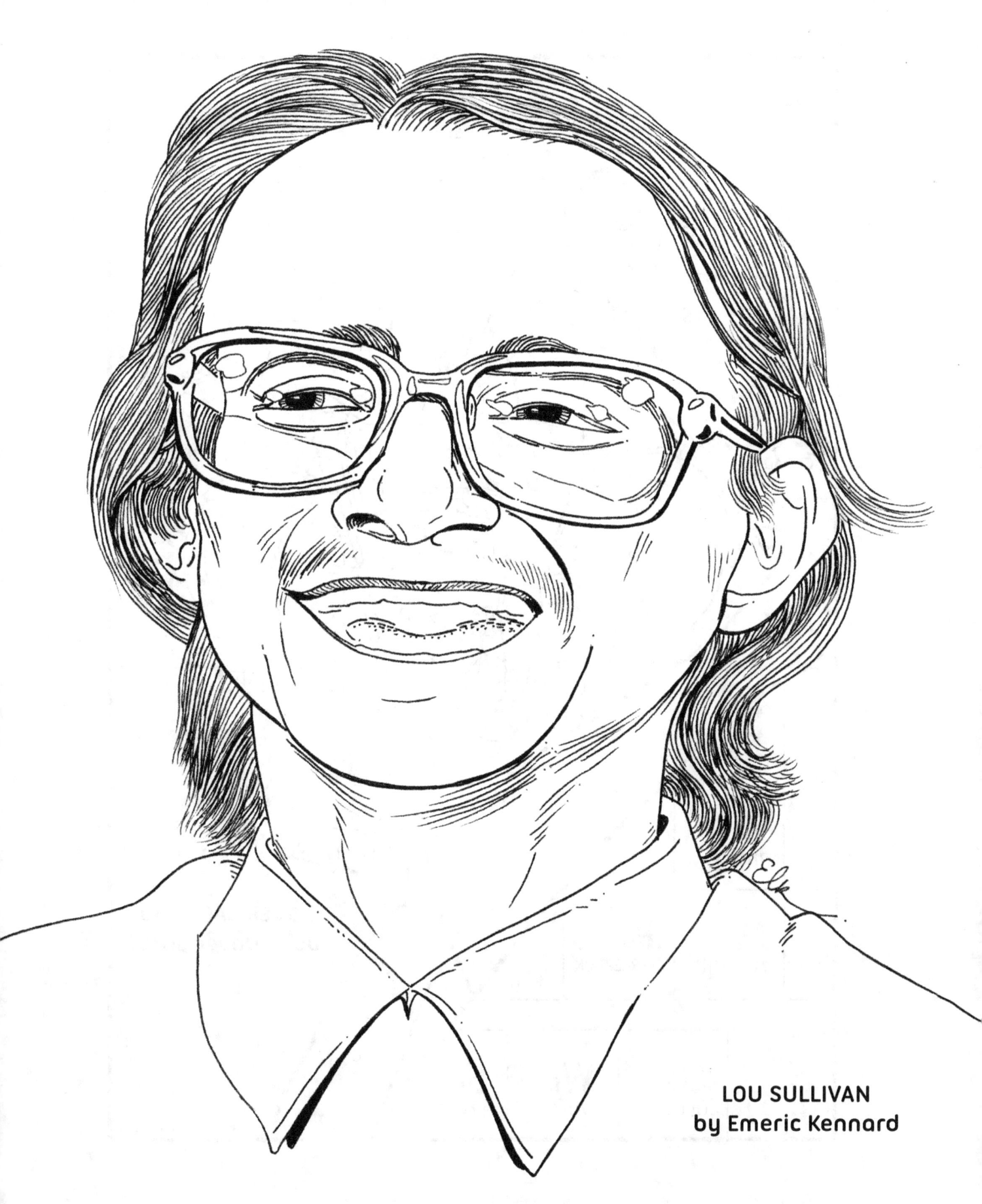

LOU SULLIVAN
by Emeric Kennard

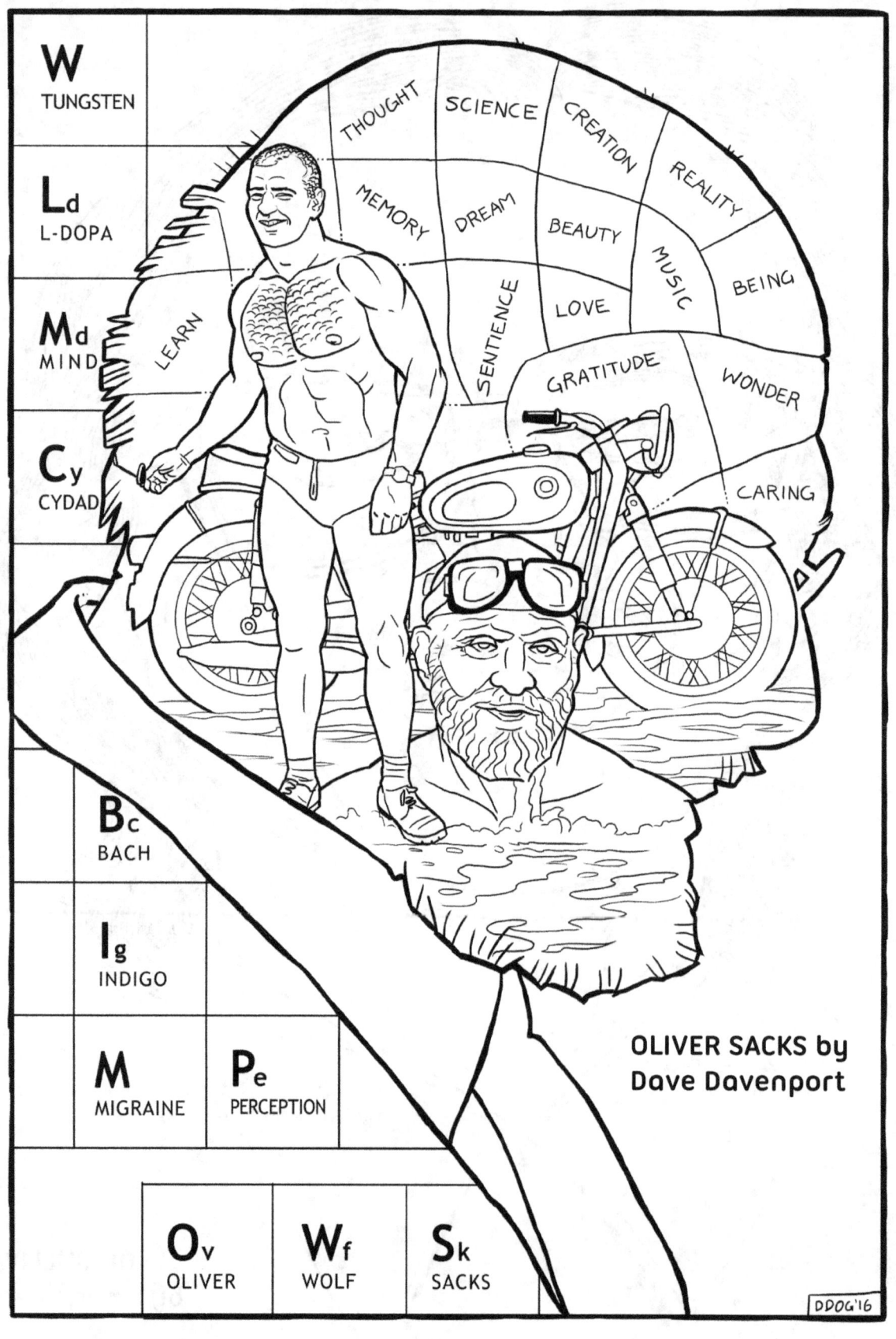

OLIVER SACKS by Dave Davenport

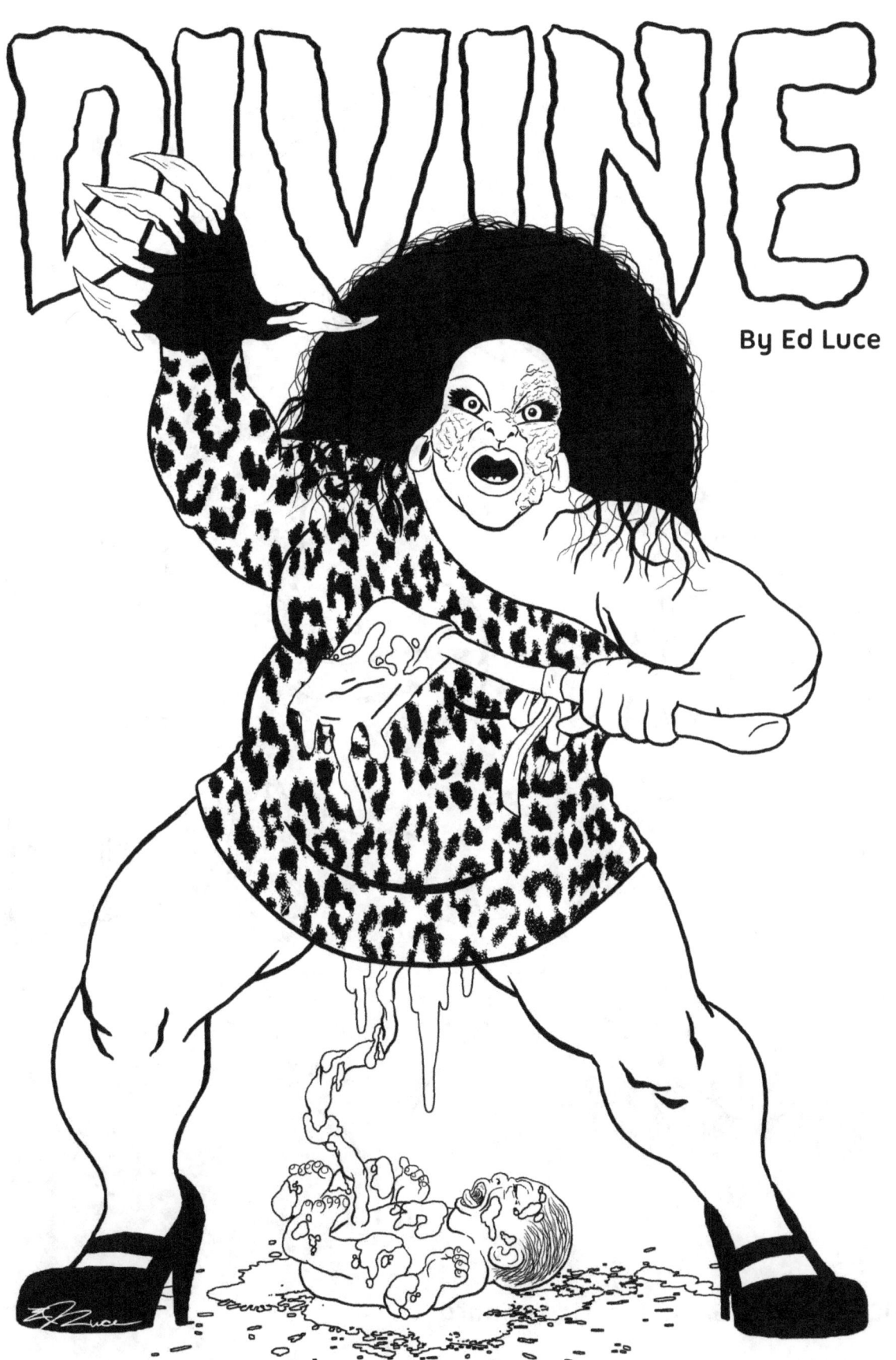

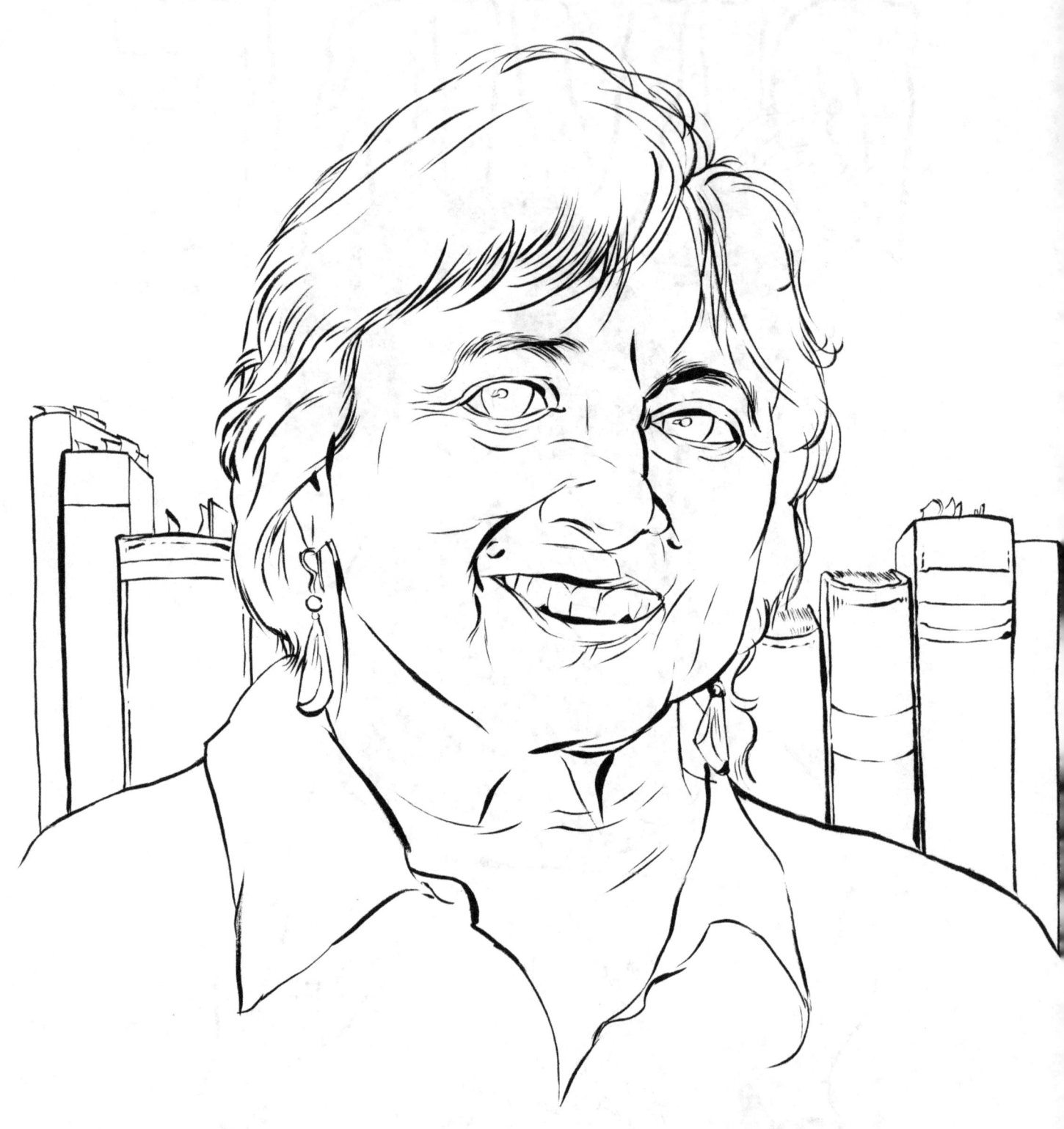

CHERRIE MORAGA by Emeric Kennard

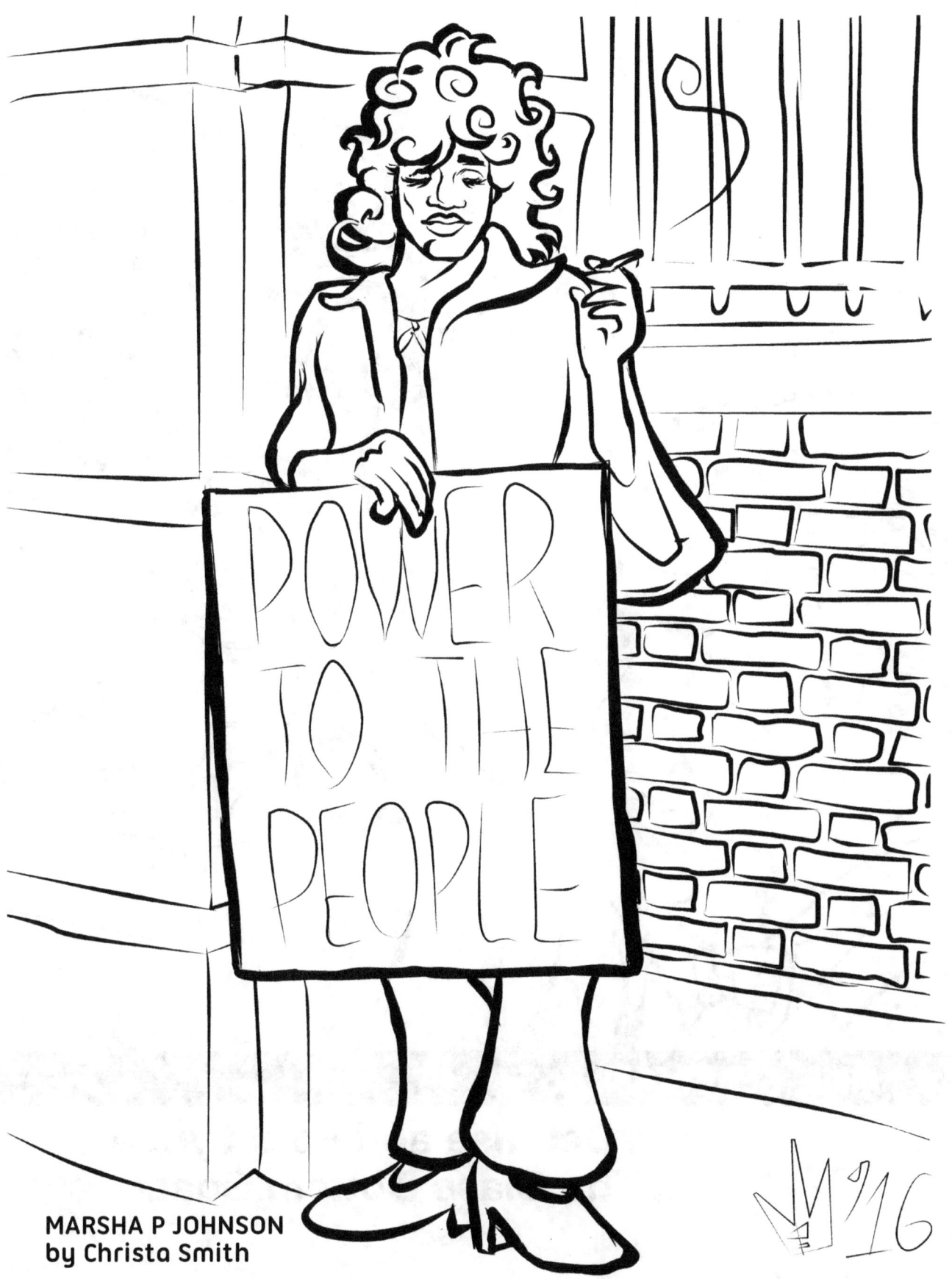

MARSHA P JOHNSON
by Christa Smith

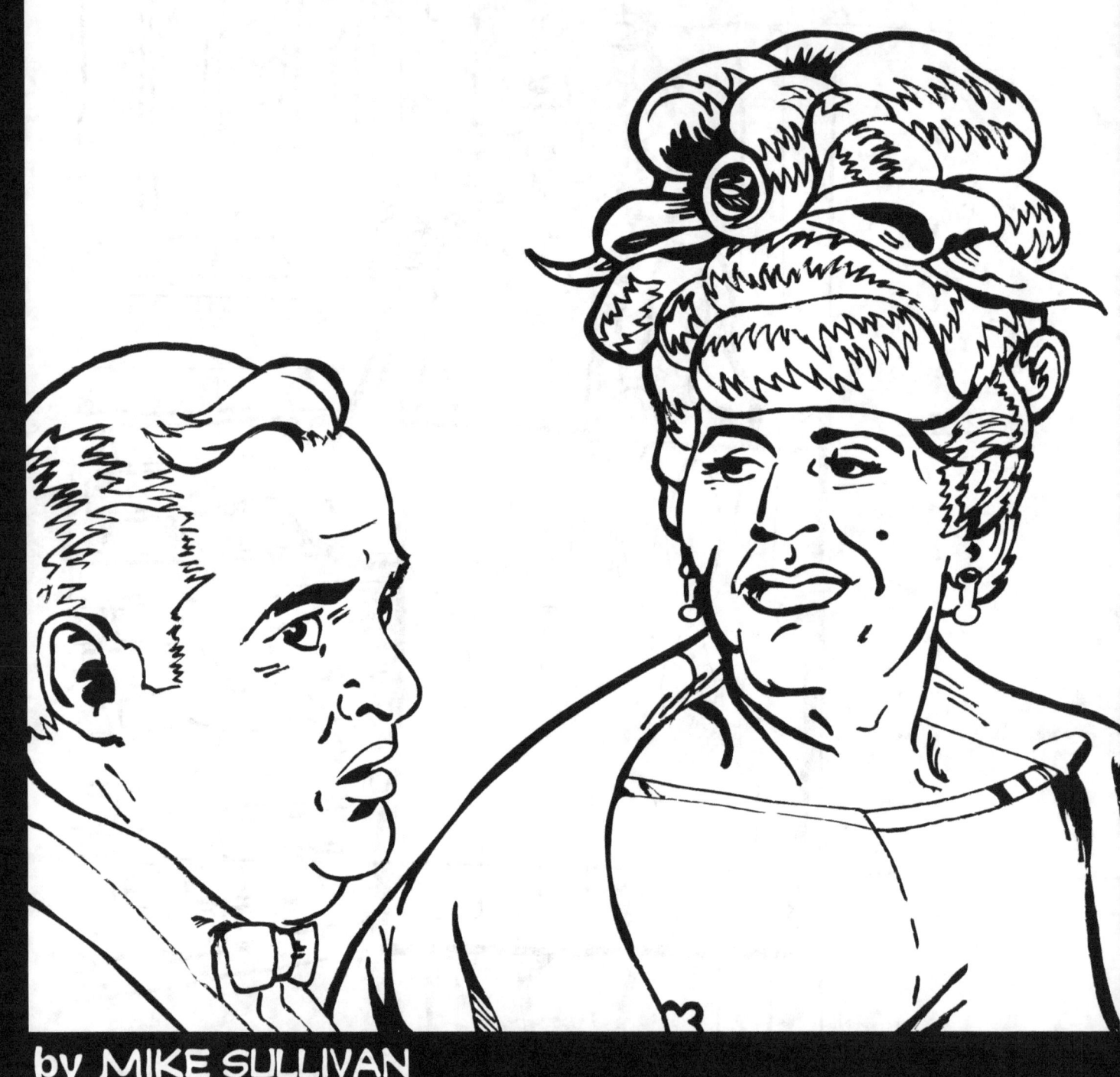

by MIKE SULLIVAN

Dom DeLuise and Paul Lynde
in The Glass Bottom Boat.

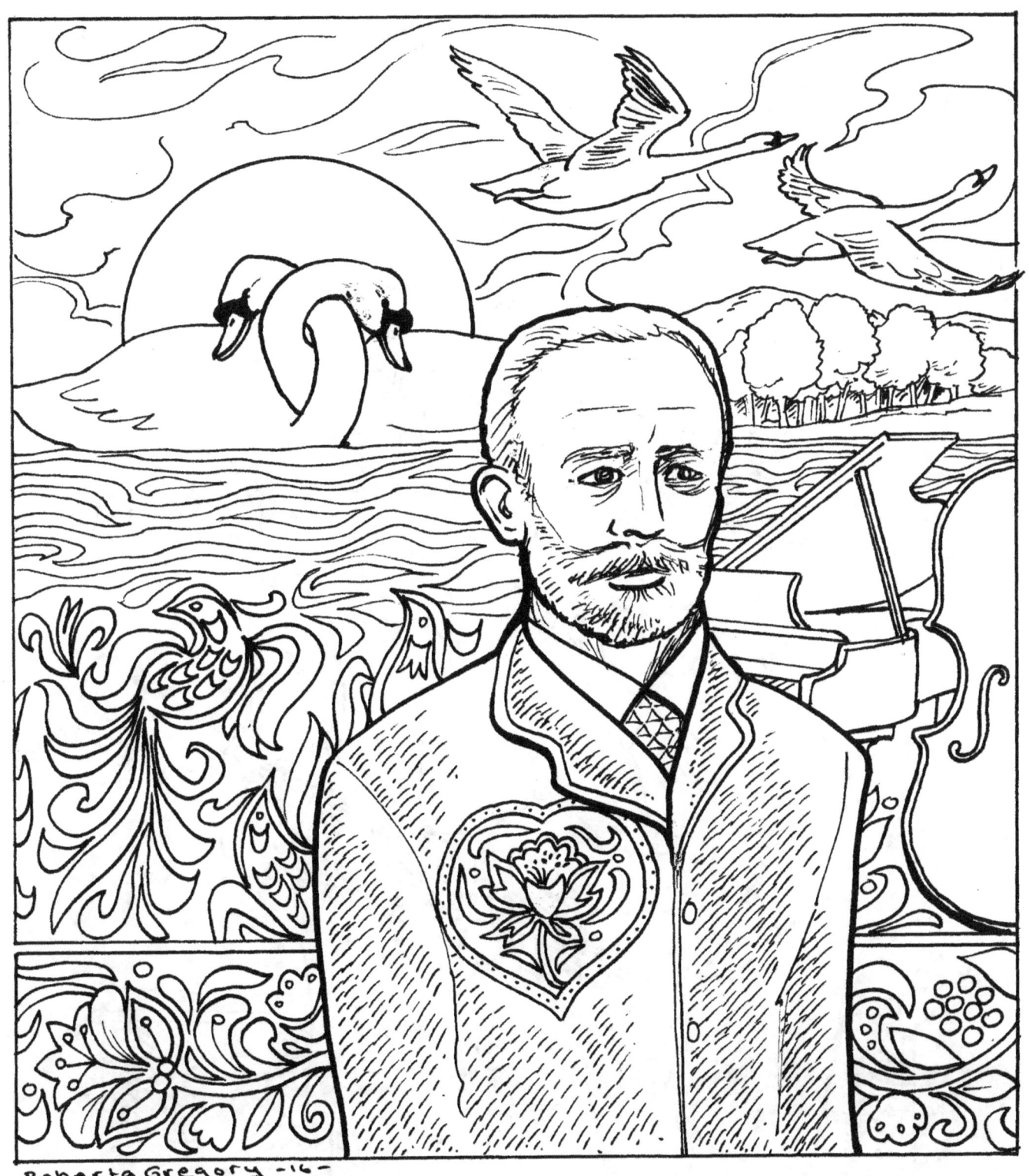

TCHAIKOVSKY by Roberta Gregory

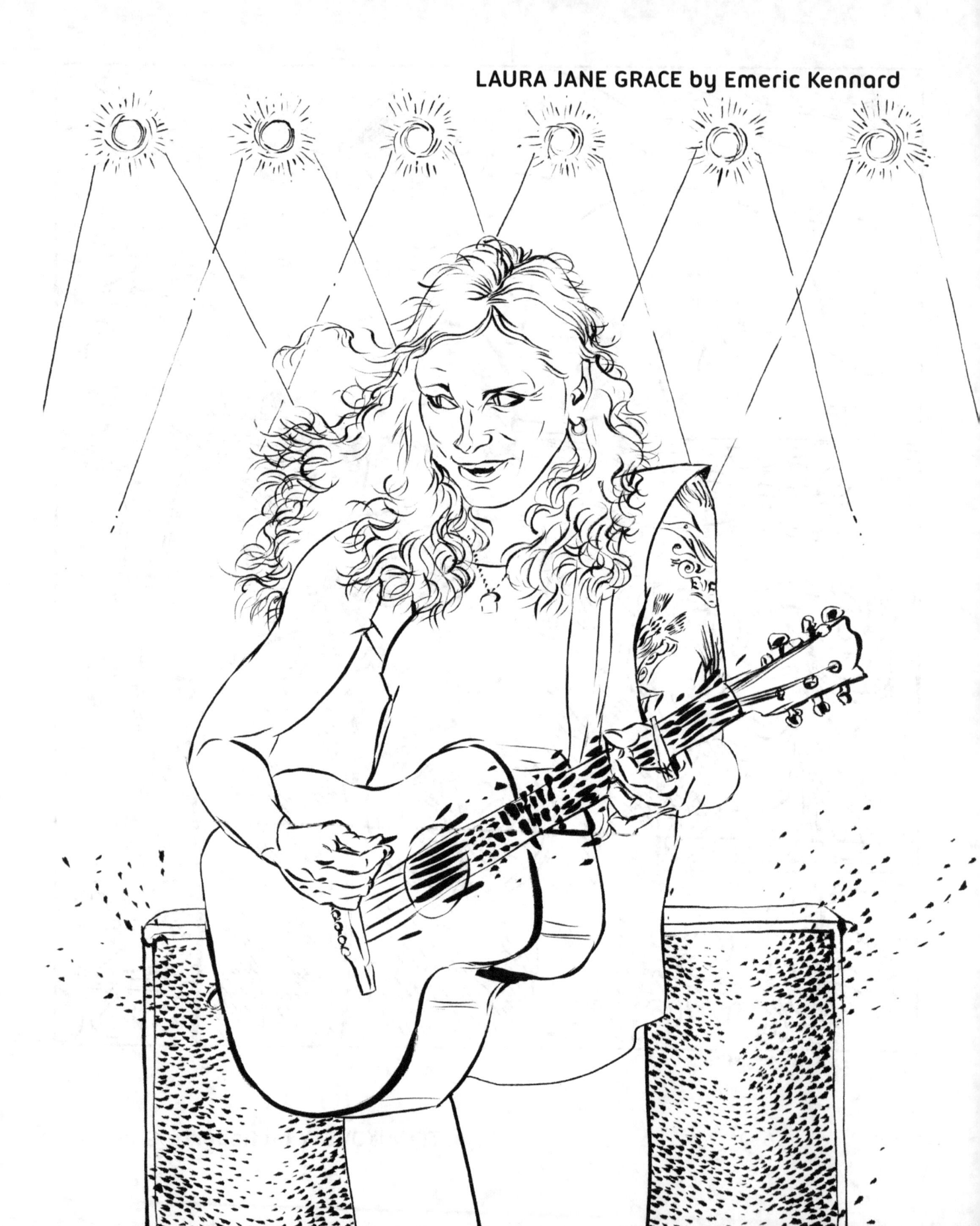

LAURA JANE GRACE by Emeric Kennard

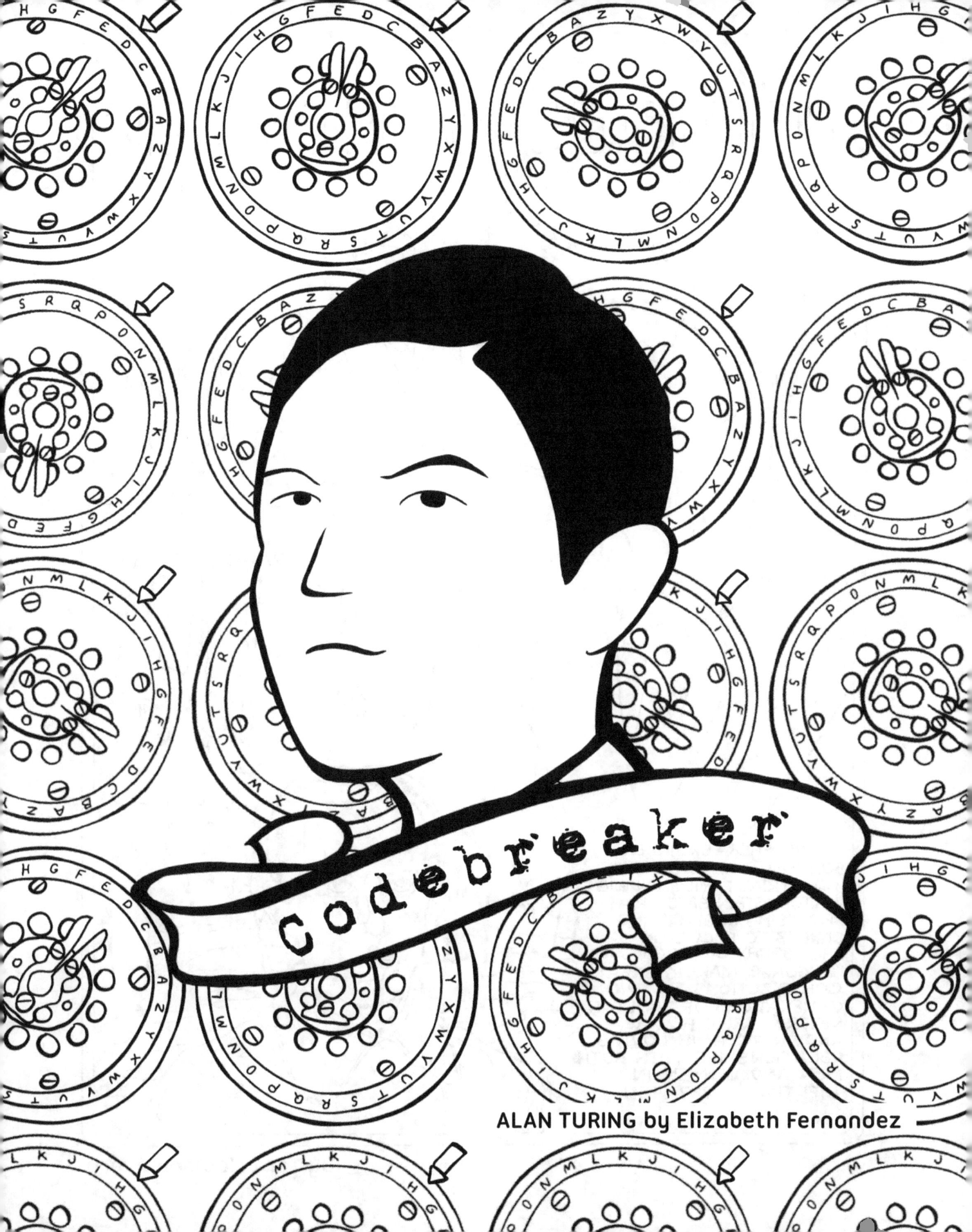

Codebreaker

ALAN TURING by Elizabeth Fernandez

ludwig.wittgenstein

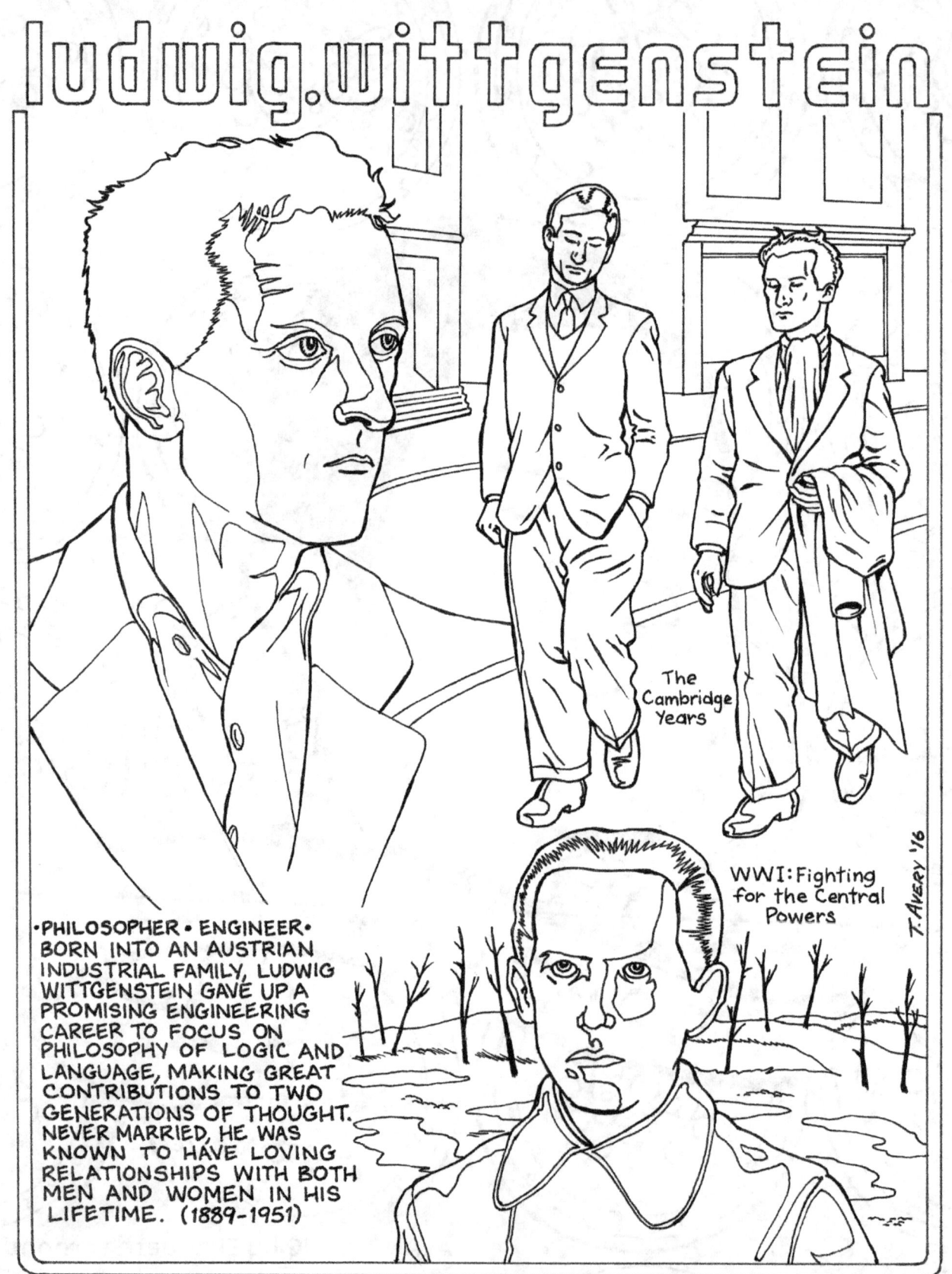

The Cambridge Years

WWI: Fighting for the Central Powers

T. Avery '16

•PHILOSOPHER • ENGINEER• BORN INTO AN AUSTRIAN INDUSTRIAL FAMILY, LUDWIG WITTGENSTEIN GAVE UP A PROMISING ENGINEERING CAREER TO FOCUS ON PHILOSOPHY OF LOGIC AND LANGUAGE, MAKING GREAT CONTRIBUTIONS TO TWO GENERATIONS OF THOUGHT. NEVER MARRIED, HE WAS KNOWN TO HAVE LOVING RELATIONSHIPS WITH BOTH MEN AND WOMEN IN HIS LIFETIME. (1889-1951)

By Tara Madison Avery

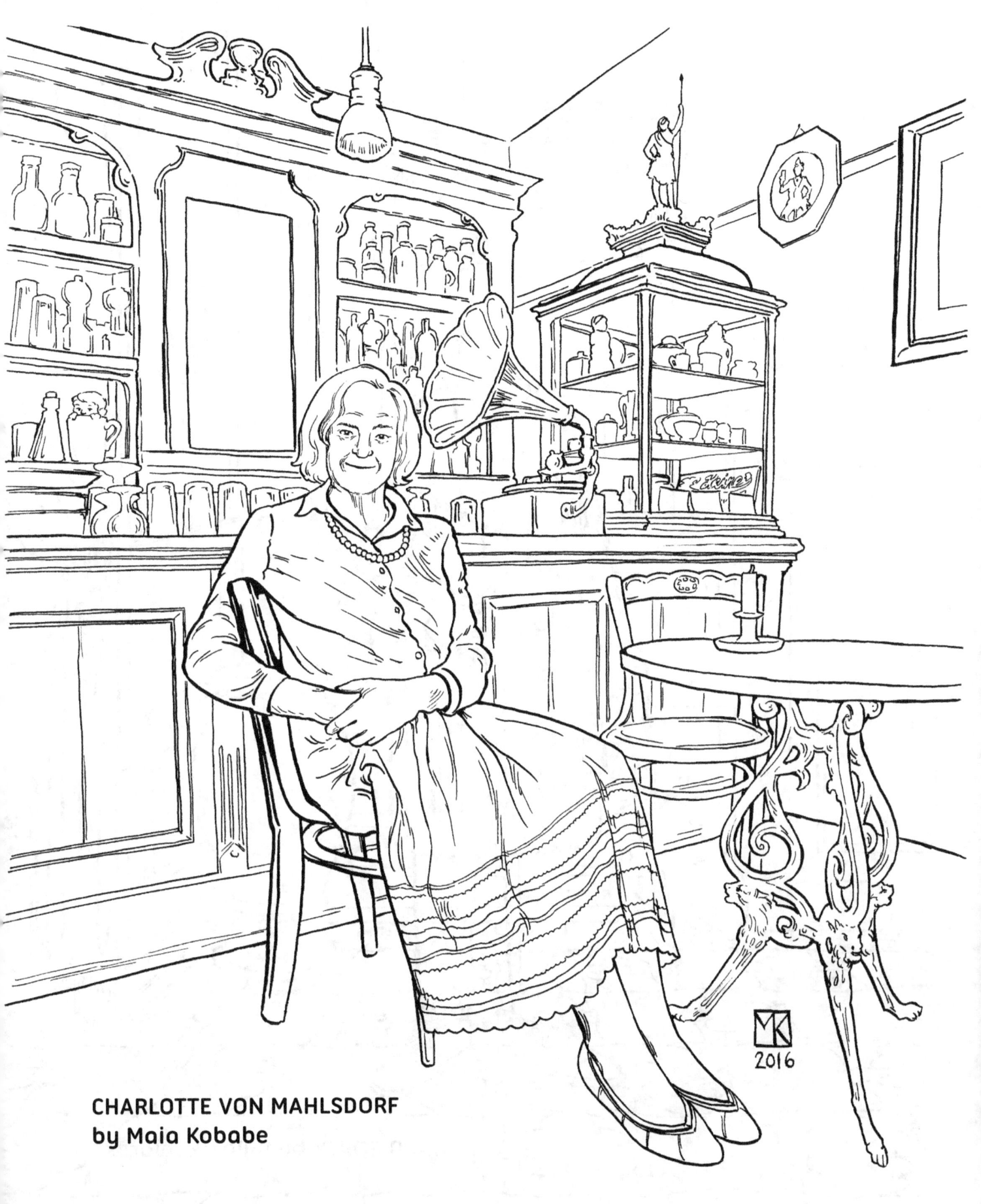

CHARLOTTE VON MAHLSDORF
by Maia Kobabe

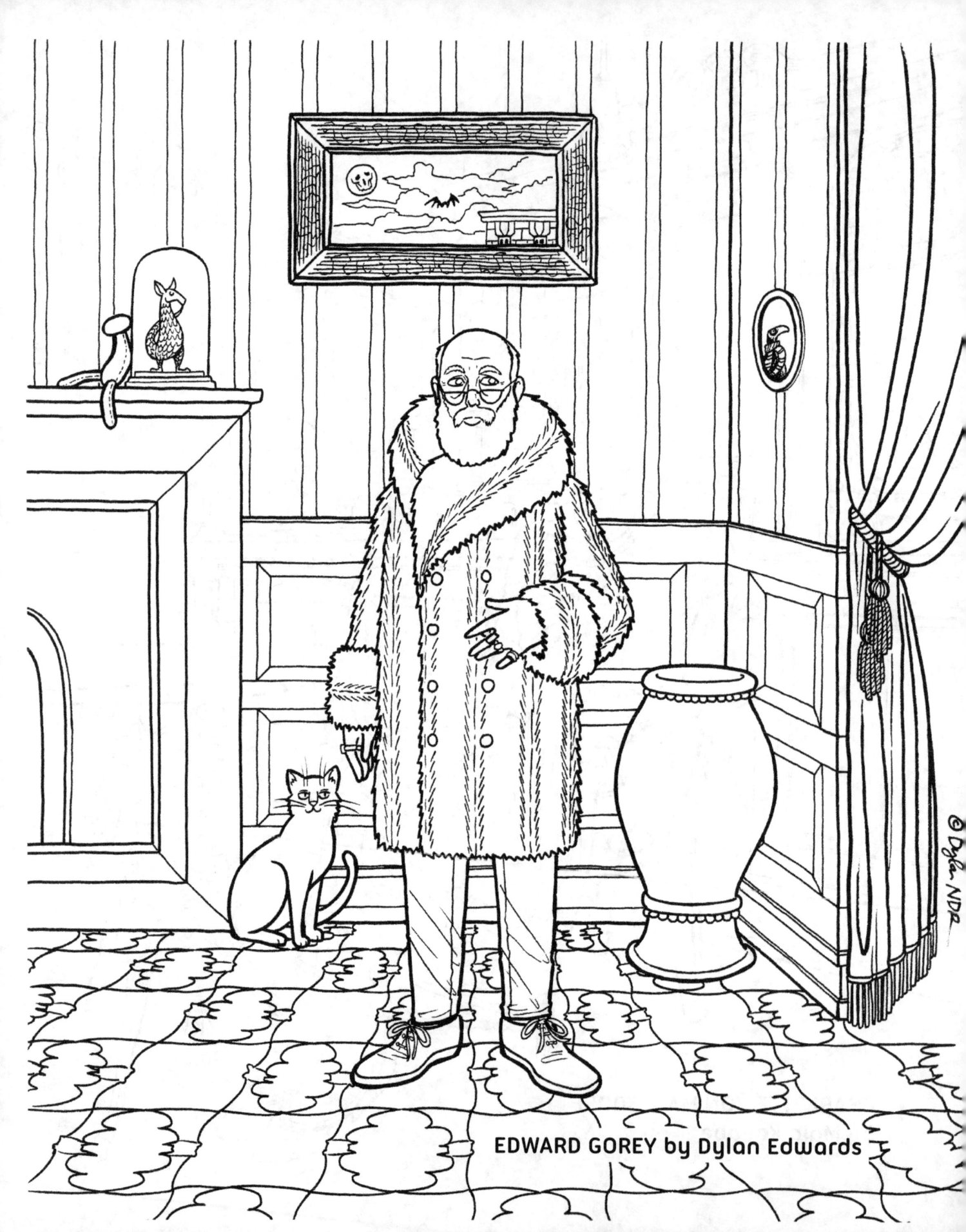

EDWARD GOREY by Dylan Edwards

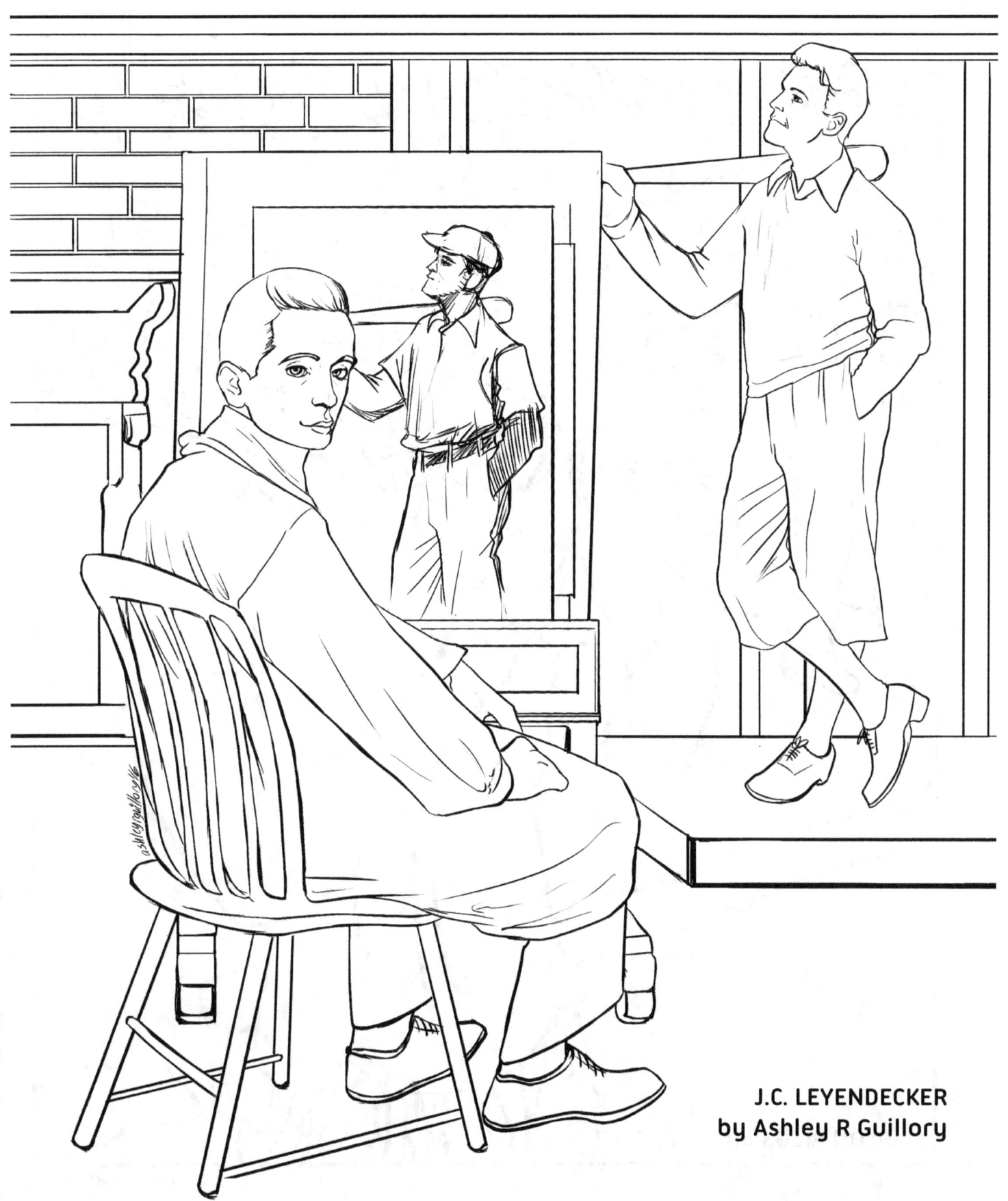

J.C. LEYENDECKER
by Ashley R Guillory

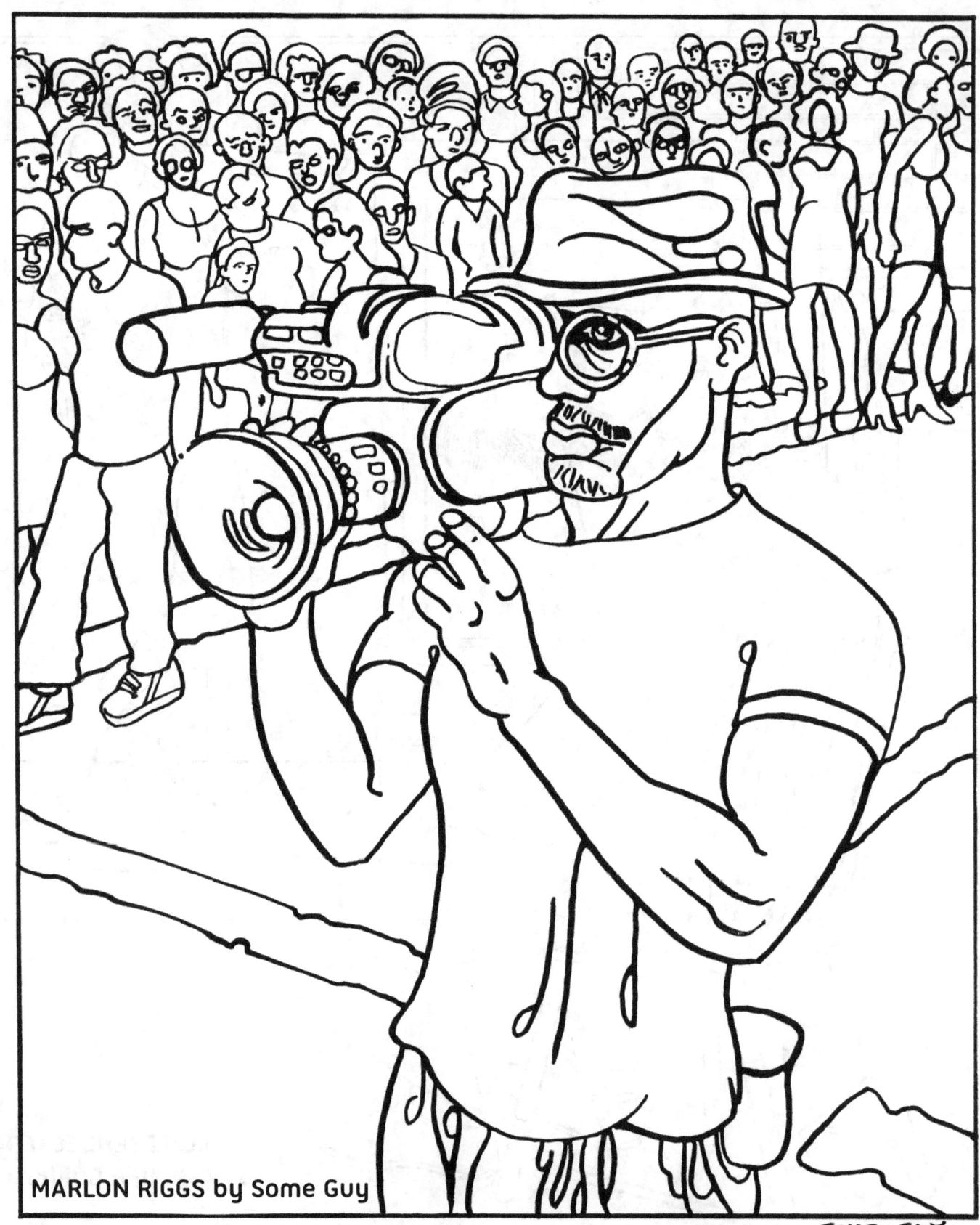

MARLON RIGGS by Some Guy

SOME GUY

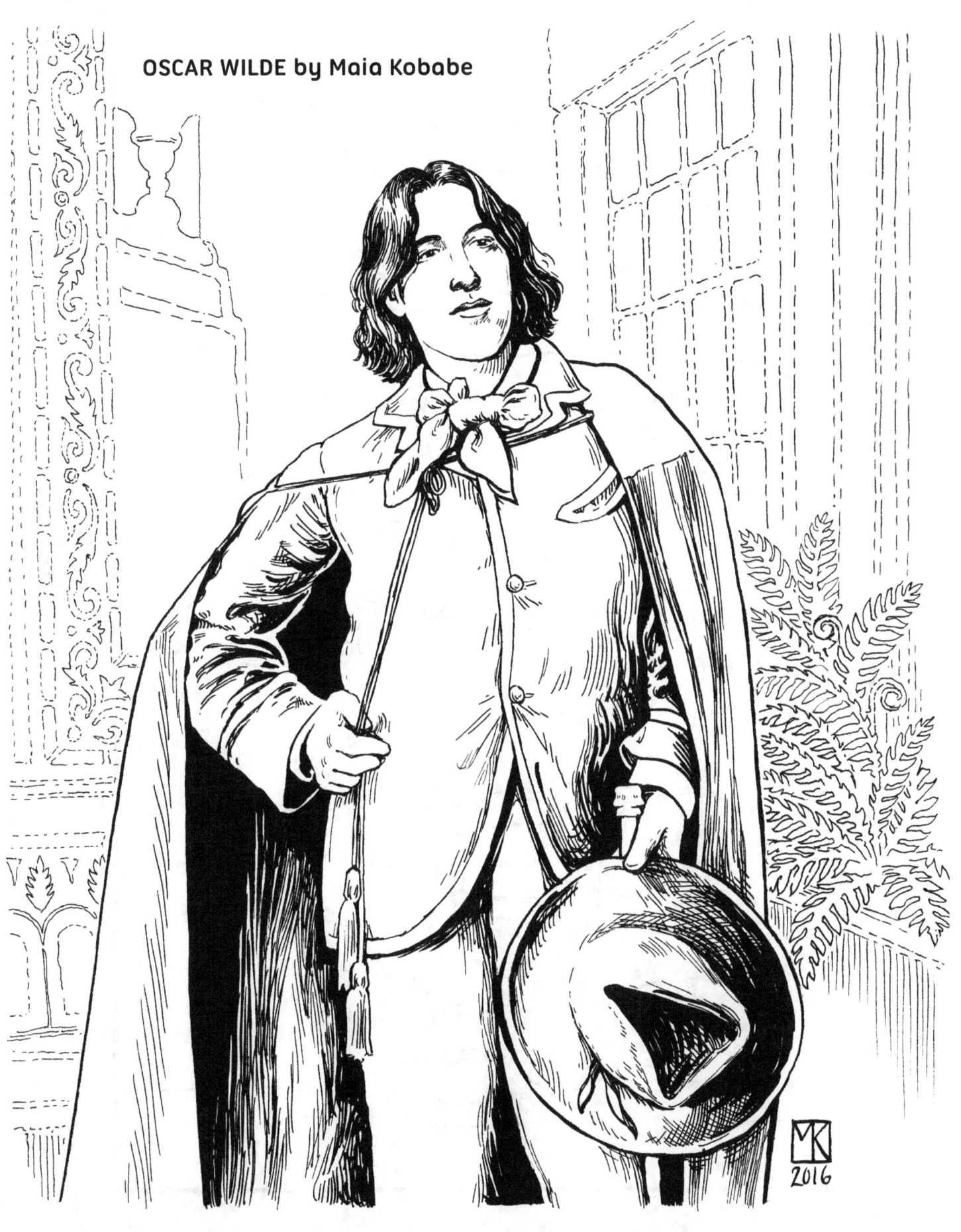

OSCAR WILDE by Maia Kobabe

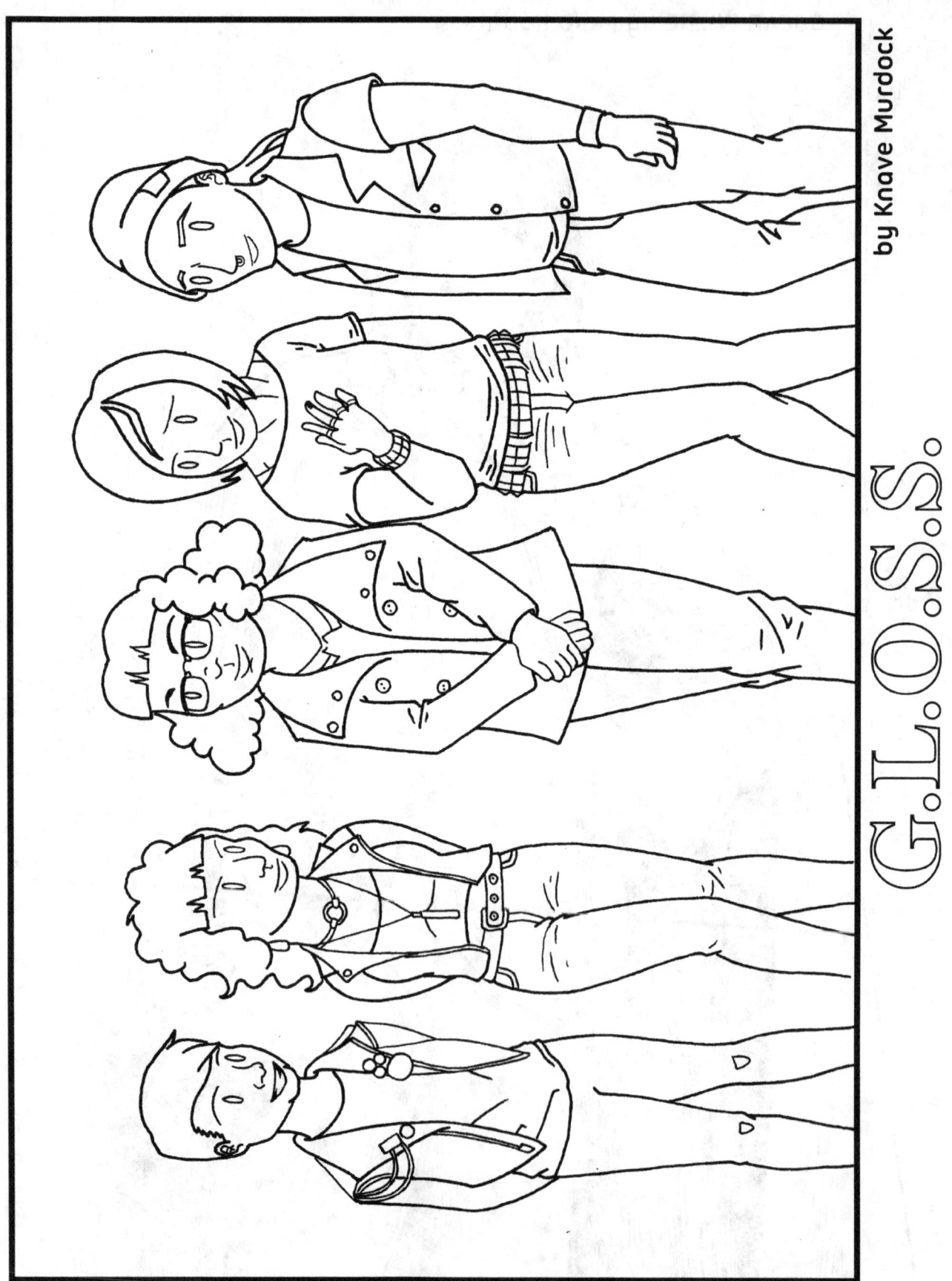

by Knave Murdock

G.L.O.S.S.

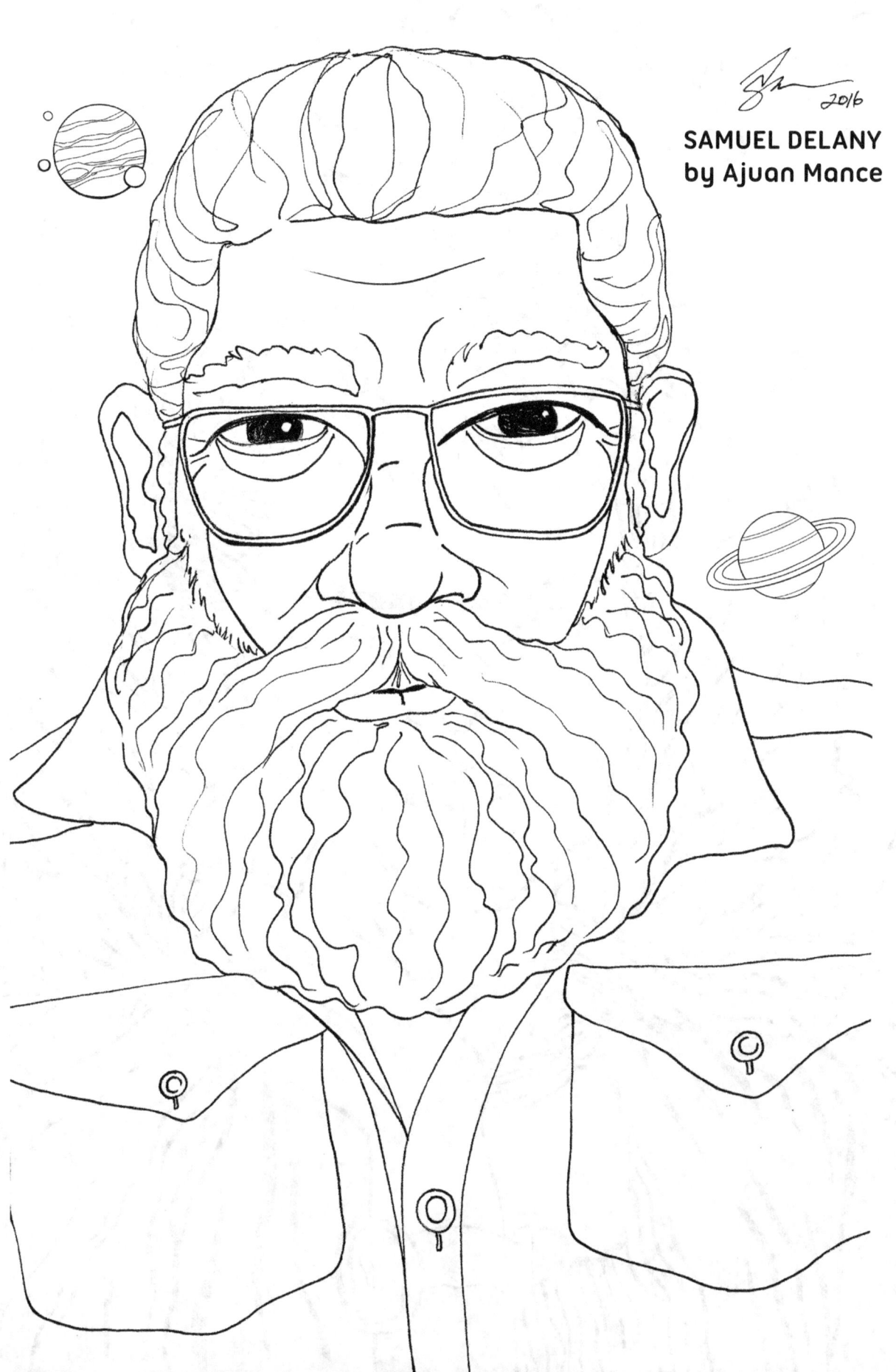

SAMUEL DELANY
by Ajuan Mance

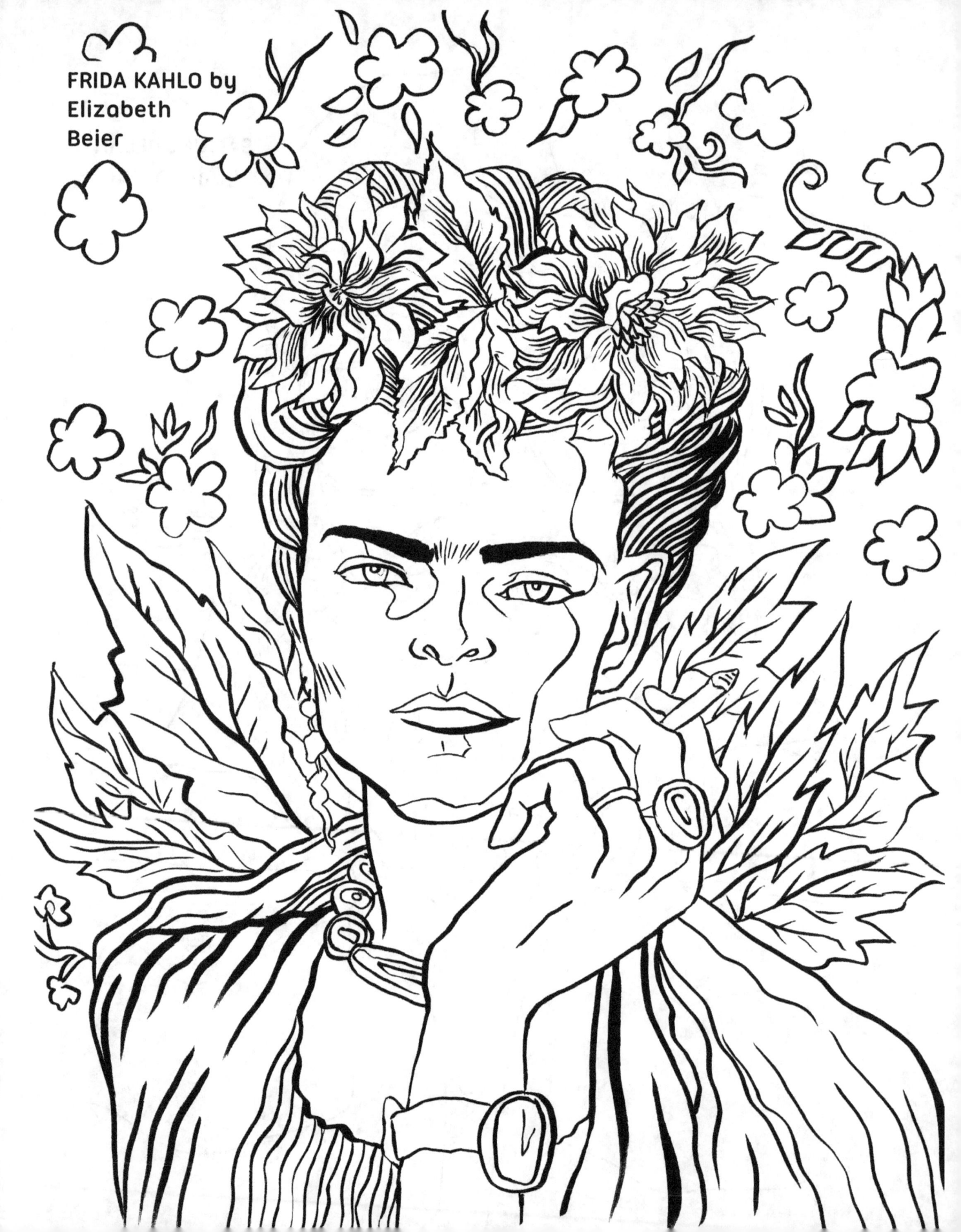

FRIDA KAHLO by
Elizabeth
Beier

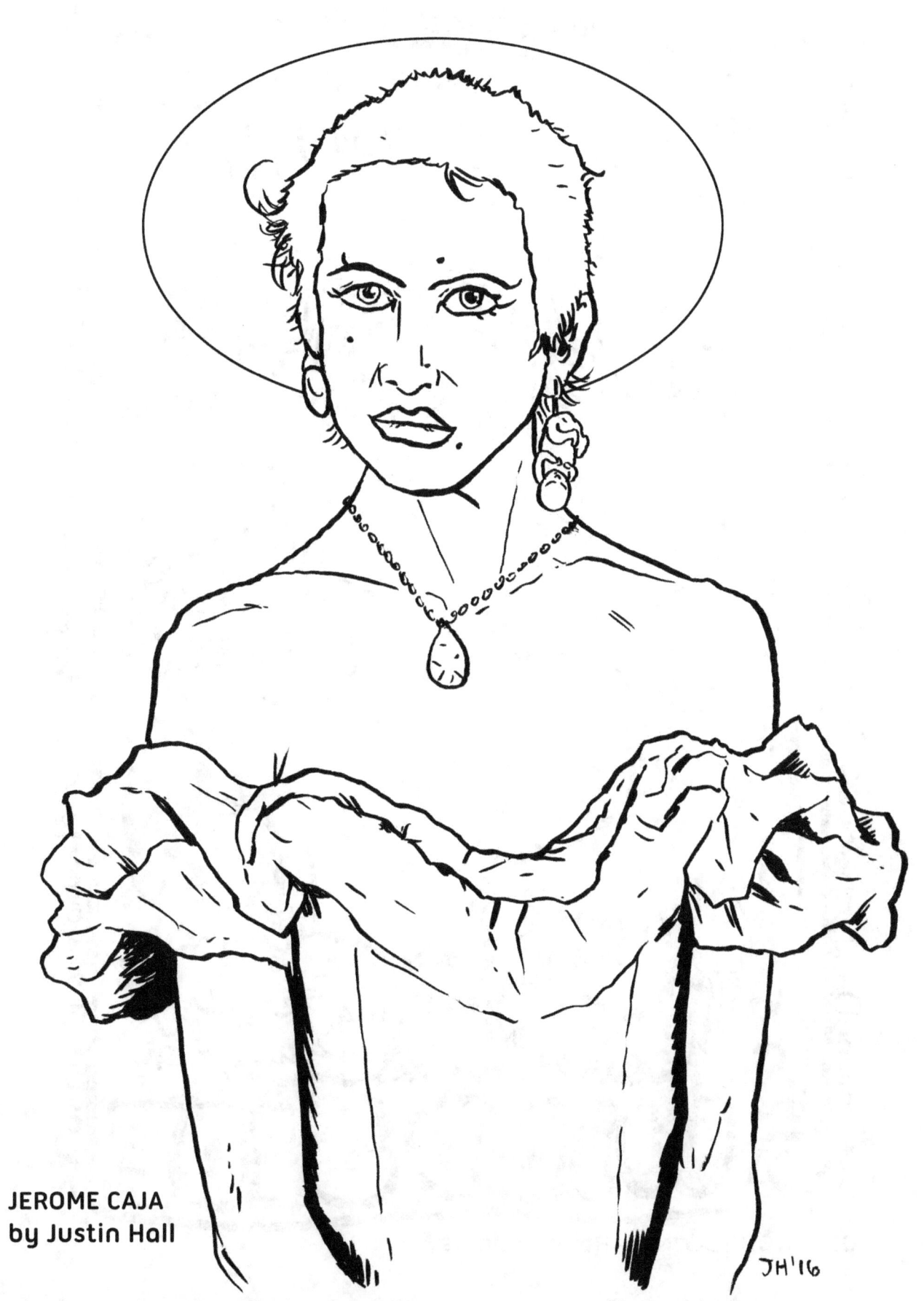

JEROME CAJA
by Justin Hall

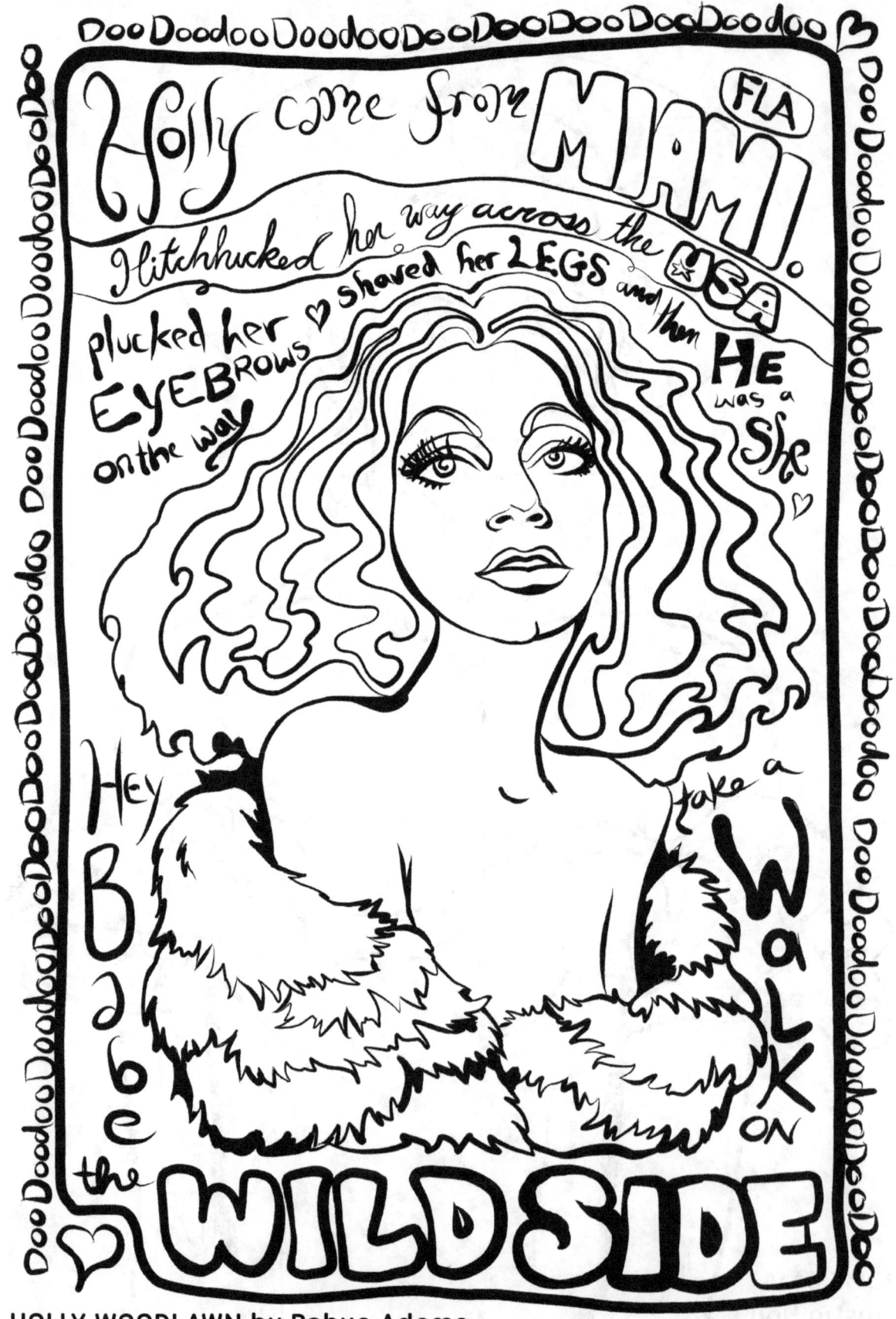

HOLLY WOODLAWN by Robyn Adams

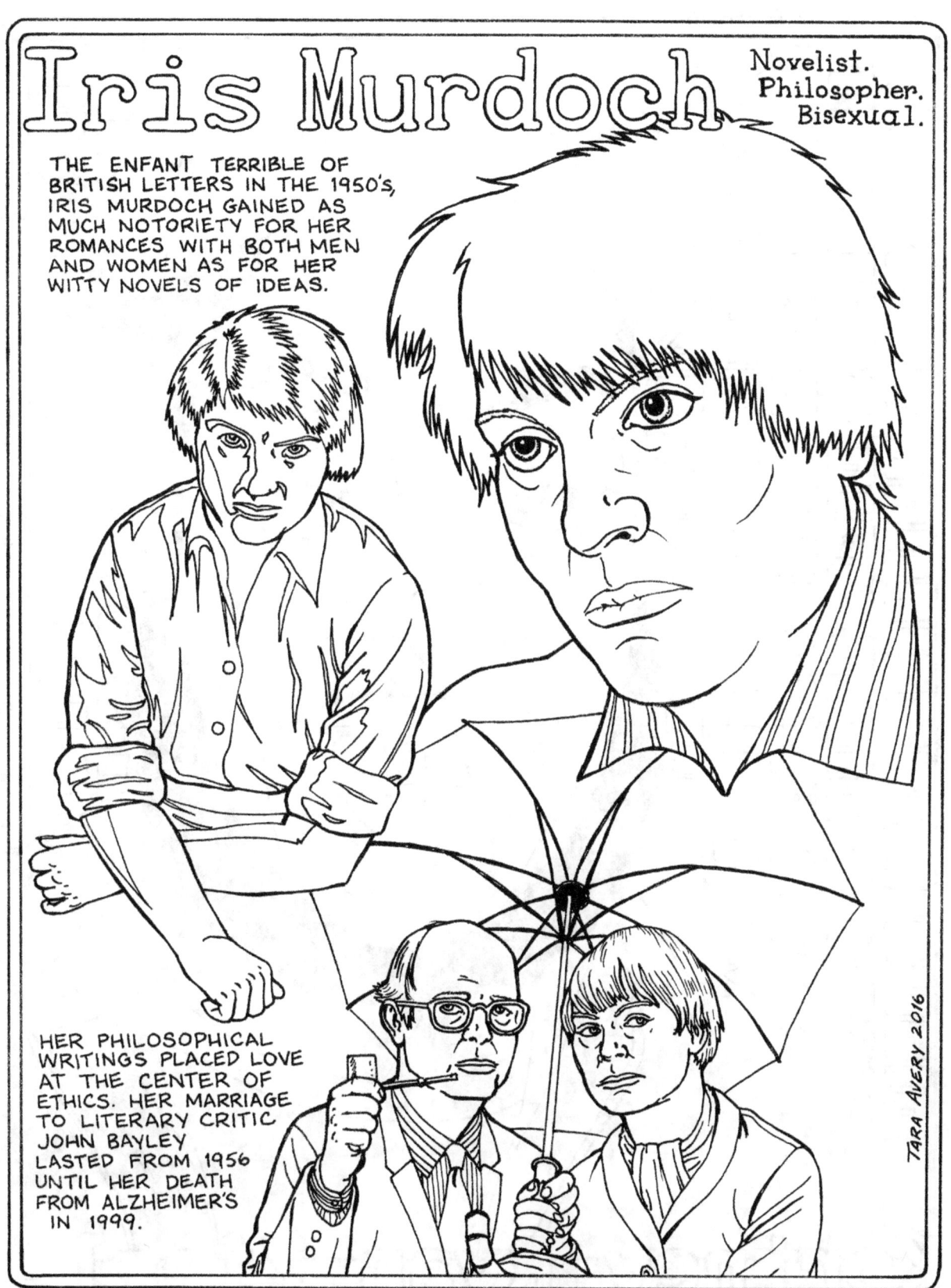

Iris Murdoch

Novelist.
Philosopher.
Bisexual.

THE ENFANT TERRIBLE OF
BRITISH LETTERS IN THE 1950's,
IRIS MURDOCH GAINED AS
MUCH NOTORIETY FOR HER
ROMANCES WITH BOTH MEN
AND WOMEN AS FOR HER
WITTY NOVELS OF IDEAS.

HER PHILOSOPHICAL
WRITINGS PLACED LOVE
AT THE CENTER OF
ETHICS. HER MARRIAGE
TO LITERARY CRITIC
JOHN BAYLEY
LASTED FROM 1956
UNTIL HER DEATH
FROM ALZHEIMER'S
IN 1999.

TARA AVERY 2016

IRIS MURDOCH by Tara Madison Avery

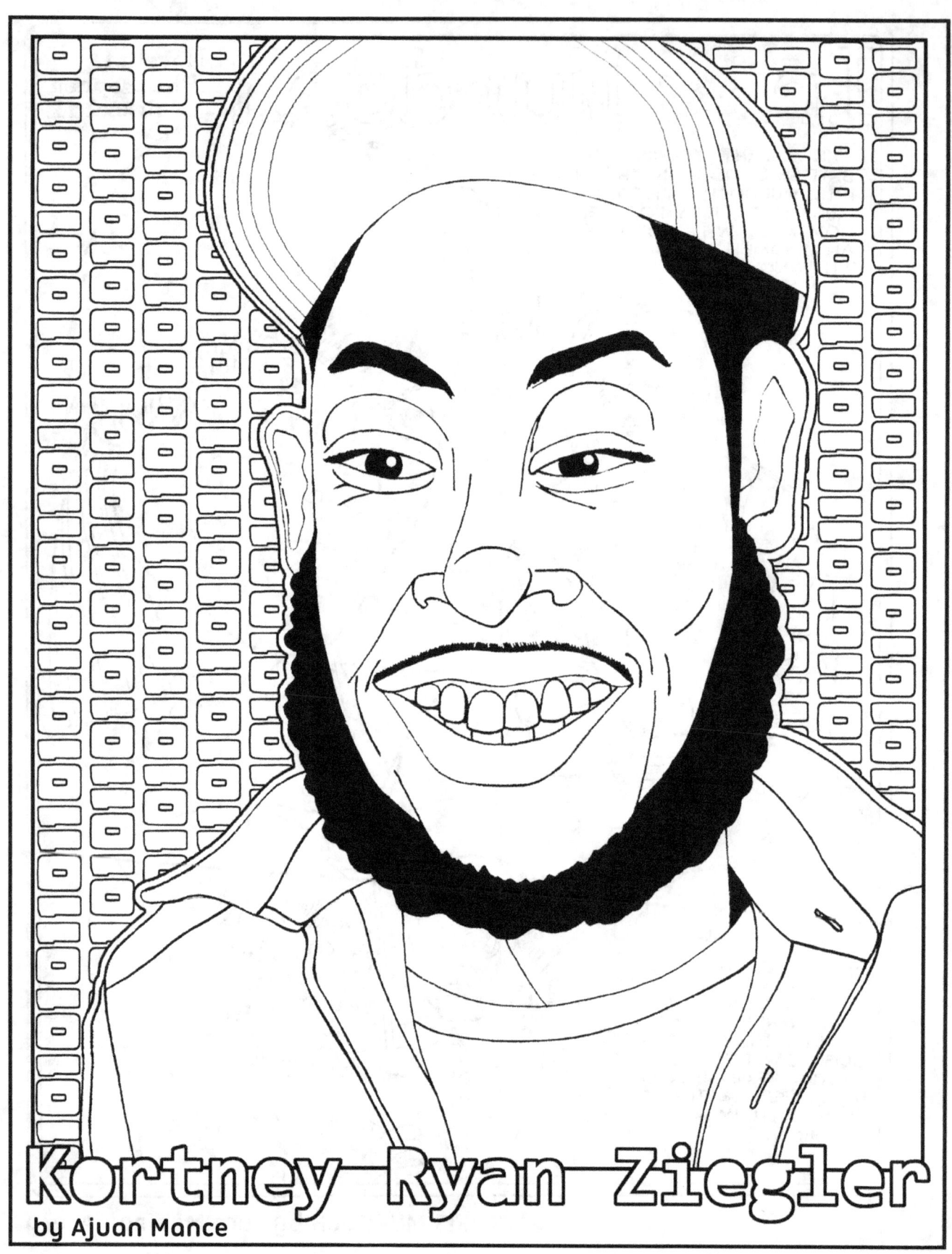

Kortney Ryan Ziegler

by Ajuan Mance

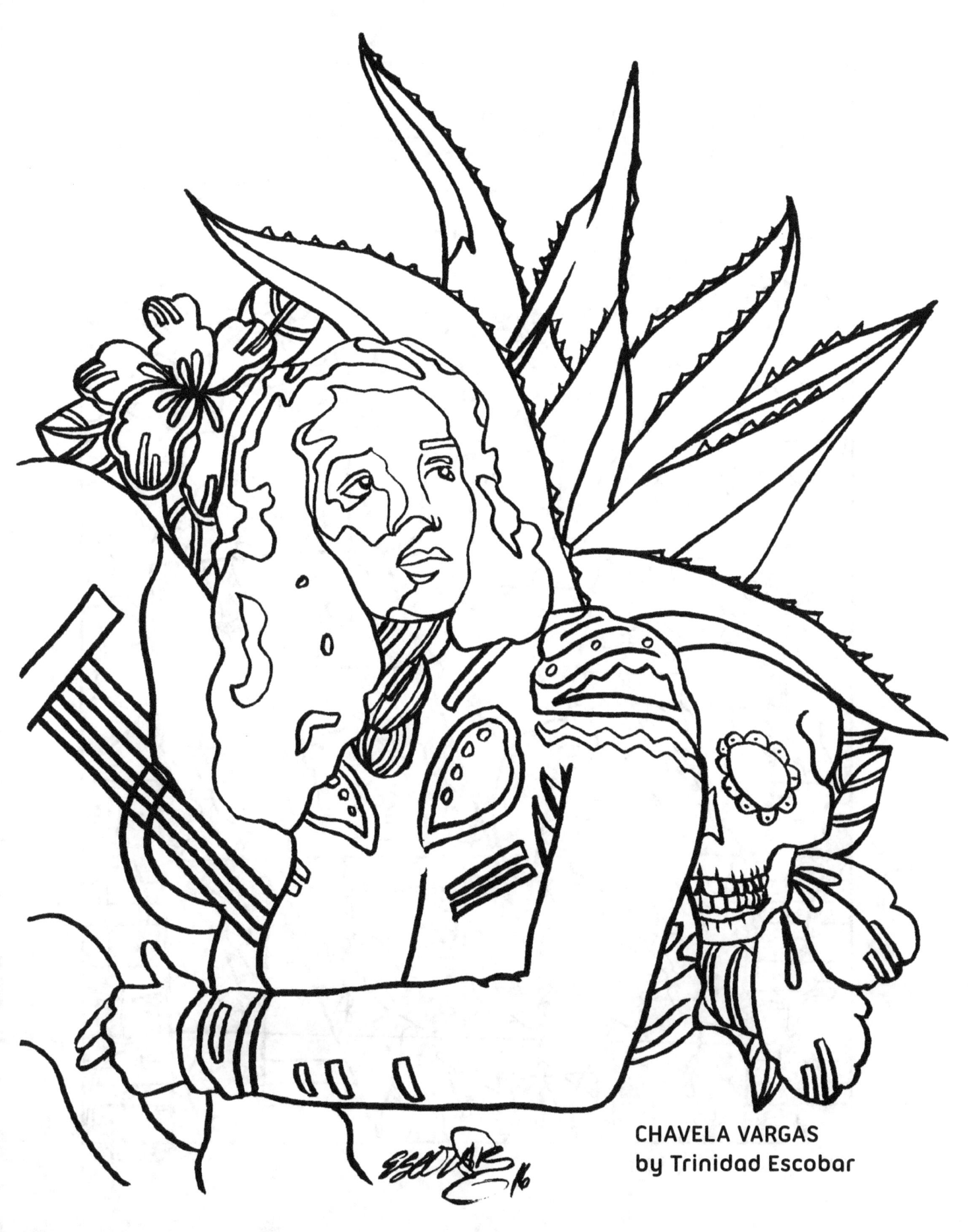

CHAVELA VARGAS
by Trinidad Escobar

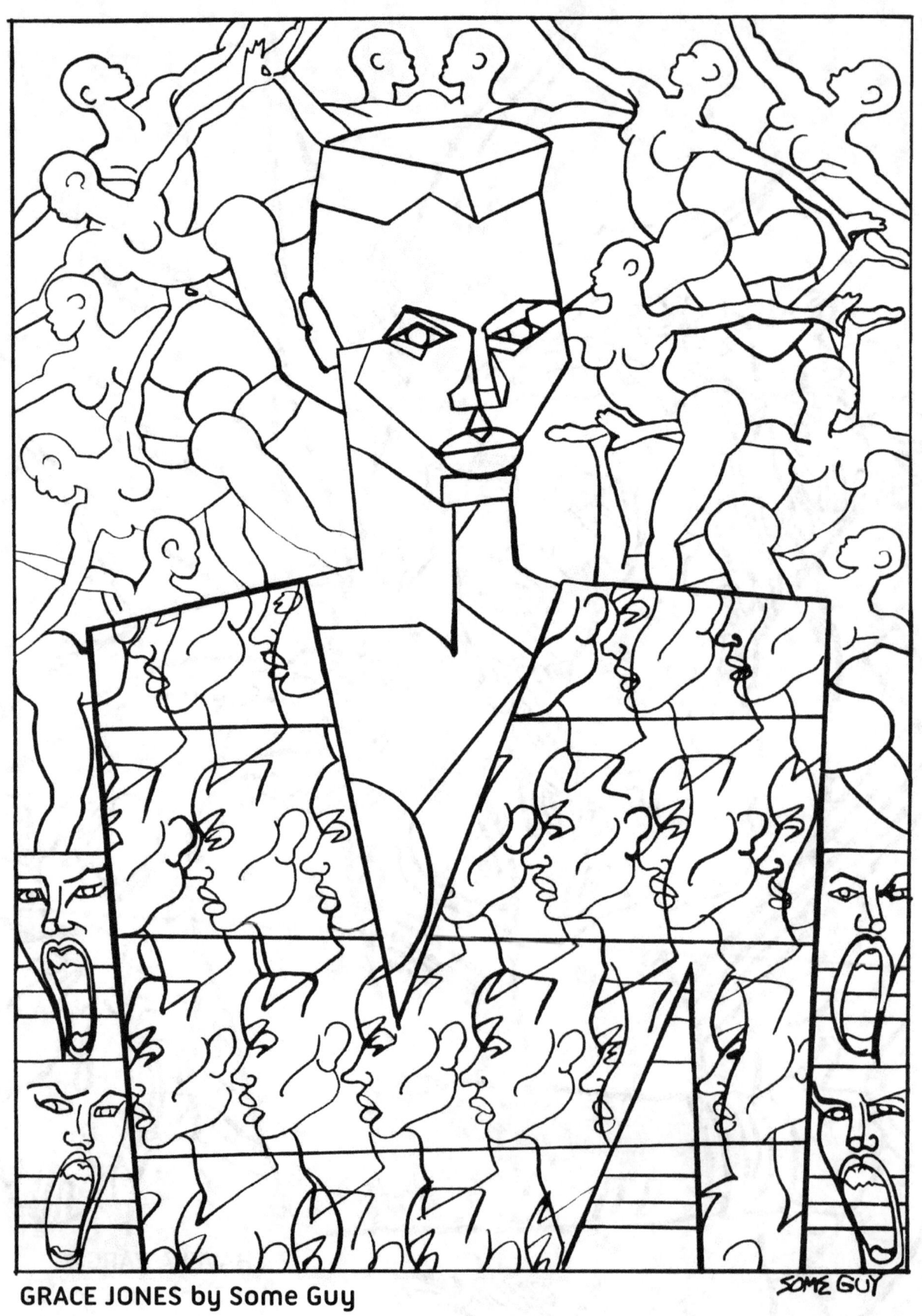

GRACE JONES by Some Guy

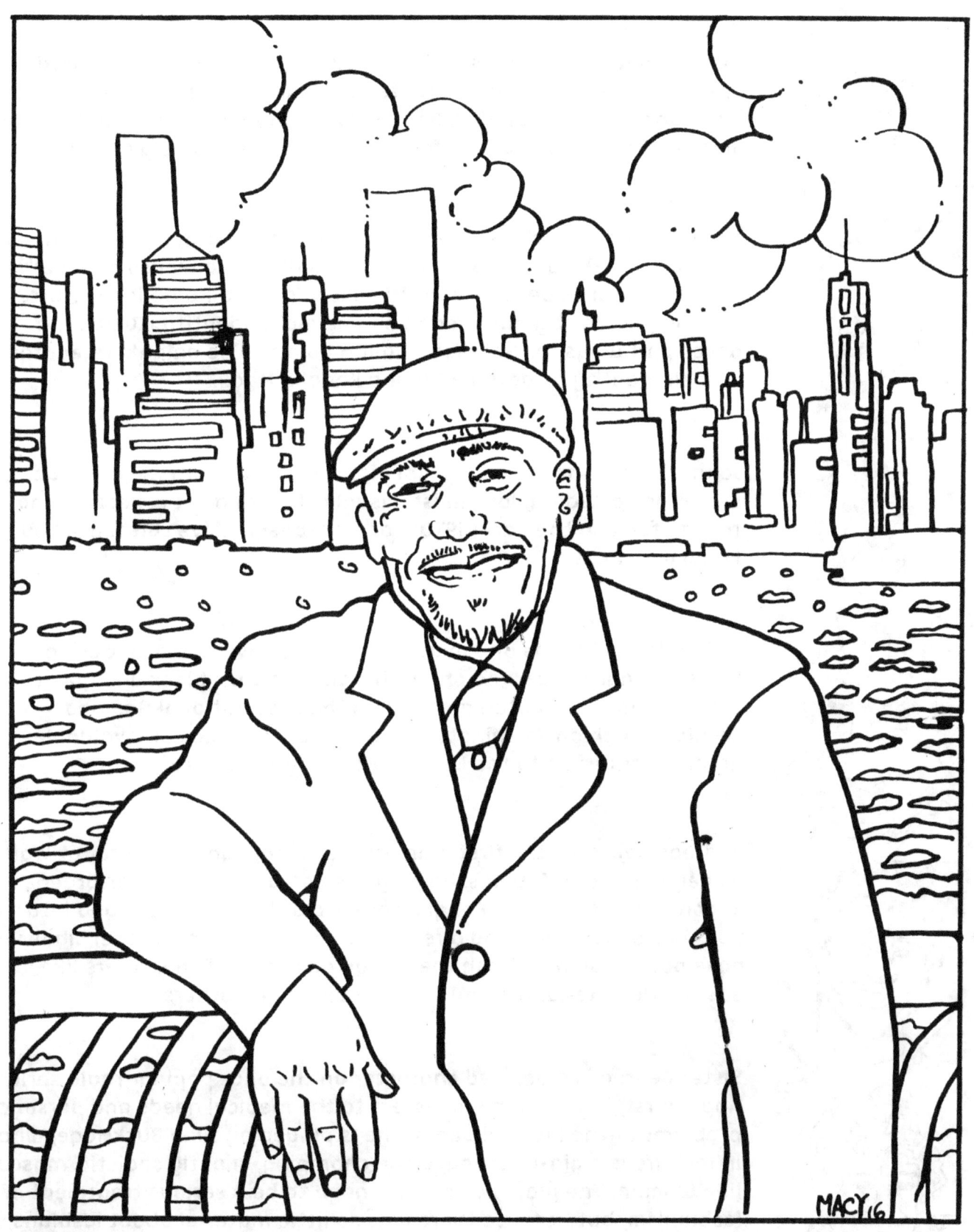

KYLAR BROADUS by Jon Macy

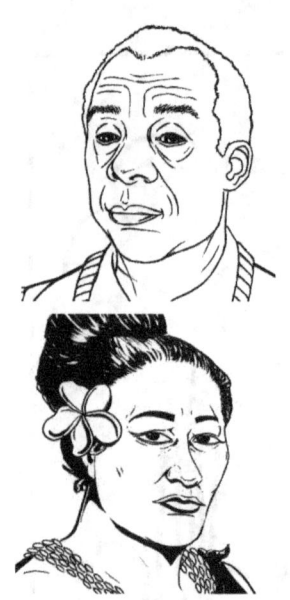

James Baldwin was an essayist, playwright, and novelist. Regarded as a highly insightful, iconic writer, with works like The Fire Next Time, and Another Country, Baldwin's second novel, Giovanni's Room, was written in 1956, well before gay rights were widely espoused in America.

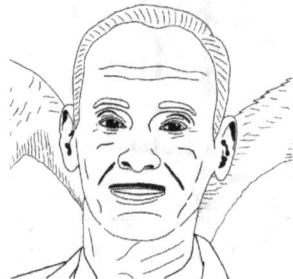

Native Hawaiian activist, educator and cultural practitioner, Hinalei-moana Wong-Kalu, best known as Kumu Hina, is a transwoman who actively reclaims gender identity as it relates to Hawaiian culture. Breaking down stigmas used to shame mahu identity, Kumu Hina paves pathways for Native Hawaiian youth to be onipa'a (steadfast) in their identity as both mahu and Kanaka Maoli.

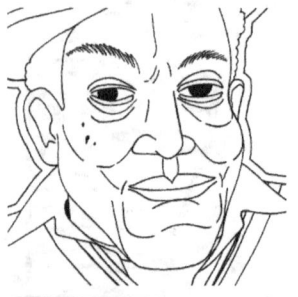

John Waters is an American film director, screenwriter, author, actor, stand-up comedian, journalist, visual artist, and art collector, who rose to fame in the early 1970s for his transgressive cult films. You know who he is.

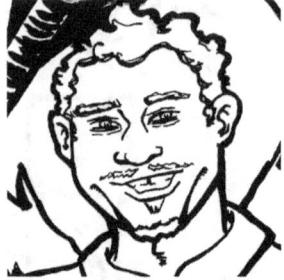

Mabel Hampton was an American lesbian activist, dancer during the Harlem Renaissance, and philanthropist for both black and queer organizations. Hampton marched in the first National Gay and Lesbian March on Washington, and has left a legacy of invaluable archival materials to the Lesbian Herstory Archives.

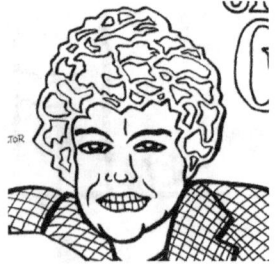

Andreas Deja was the first high profile, openly gay animator at Walt Disney Animation Studios, helping the company strike a resurgence in popularity during its Renaissance era of the late 1980s and into the 90s. As a supervising and directing animator, his specific sensibilities have been shown through the design and form of characters like Gaston, Hercules and King Triton, among many others.

Sister George is a beloved character on the once popular radio series Applehurst, a nurse who ministers to the medical needs and personal problems of the local villagers. She is played by June Buckridge, who in real life is a gin-guzzling, cigar-chomping, slightly sadistic, mascu-line woman. The play was not intended to be a serious treatment of lesbianism, but because there was so little material about lesbians, it became treated as such.

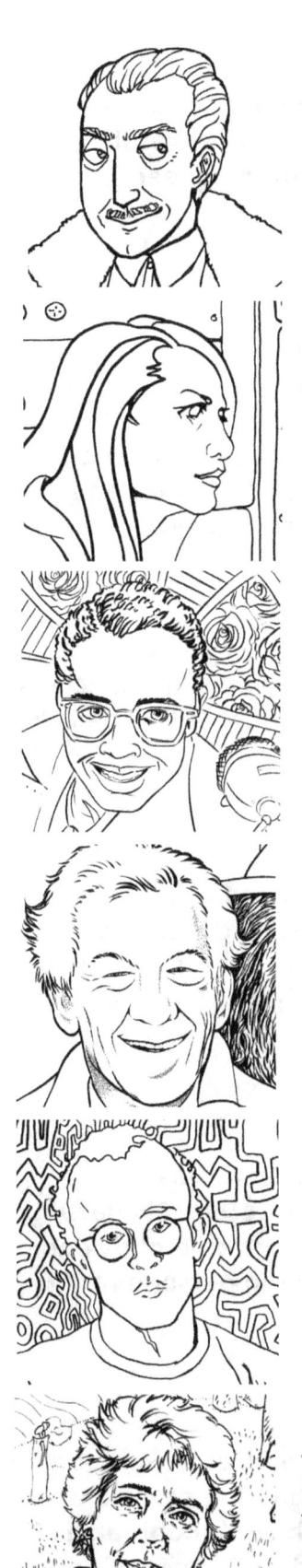

Tom of Finland was a Finnish artist, notable for his stylized homo erotic fetish art and his influence on late twentieth century gay culture. He holds a special place as the great grand daddy of all queer artists of masculinity.

Wendy Carlos is an American composer and keyboardist best known for her electronic music and film scores. Carlos performed on a Moog synthesizer, which helped popularize its use in the 1970s, and won her three Grammy Awards. She composed the scores for A Clockwork Orange, The Shining, and Tron. She is made 100% of the awesome.

Wilmer Broadnax was born in Houston. Both he and his brother, Big Axe, were singers. Broadnax developed a strong tenor voice. In the mid '40s, they moved to Southern California to advance their singing careers. It was not known that he was a trans man until the time of his death.

Sir Ian McKellen is an English actor. In 1988, he came out to the general public on a BBC Radio program in protest of the controversial Section 28 of the Local Government Bill. Section 28 proposed prohibiting local authorities from promoting homosexuality. McKellen is a co-founder of Stonewall, an LGBT rights lobby group in the United Kingdom. He's tops.

Keith Haring was an American artist and social activist, whose work responded to the New York City street culture of the 1980s. Haring's work was often heavily political. The theme of AIDS featured greatly in Haring's later works. His imagery has become a widely recognized visual language of the 20th century.

Joanna Russ was an American writer, academic, and radical feminist. She is the author of a number of works of science fiction, fantasy, and feminist literary criticism, such as How to Suppress Women's Writing, On Strike Against God, and one children's book, Kittatinny. She is best known for The Female Man.

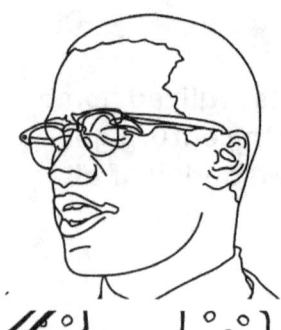

Researchers claim that Malcolm X engaged in a myriad of same-sex relationships and was bisexual. It is also claimed that several African- American activists have tried to cover up the queer history of this leader.

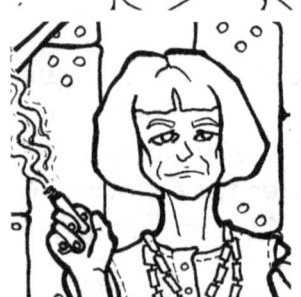

Jane Bowles was an author, bisexual, alcoholic, and womanizer. She is best known for the novel Two Serious Ladies, and the play In the Summer House. She was married to the bisexual composer, Paul Bowles. Paul and Jane spent several years in Morocco, where Paul introduced Jane to Cherifa. Cherifa was a butch Moroccan woman who sold grains in the souk and practiced witchcraft. Rumor had it that Cherifa poisoned Jane, a rumor that Jane encouraged.

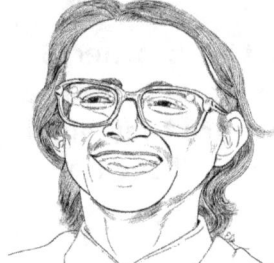

Lou Sullivan was a leading activist in the grassroots female-to-male (FTM) movement. He was instrumental in increasing visibility, access to transitional and mental healthcare, and peer support for the FTM community.

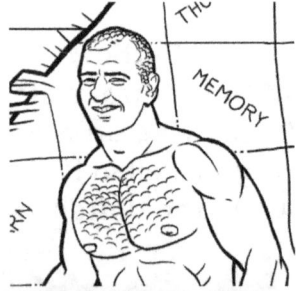

Oliver Sacks was a British neurologist, naturalist, and author. Sacks never married and lived alone for most of his life. He declined to share details from his personal life until he addressed his homosexuality for the first time in his 2015 autobiography, On the Move: A Life.

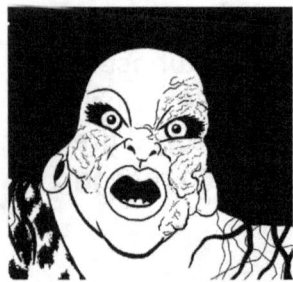

Divine was an American actor, singer, and drag queen. Closely associated with the independent filmmaker John Waters, Divine was a character actor, usually performing female roles in cinematic and theatrical appearances, and adopting a female drag persona for his music career.

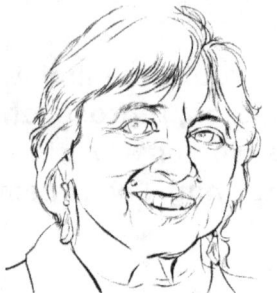

Cherríe Moraga is a Chicana writer, activist, and educator. Her work has been foundational to concepts of intersectionality, especially for queer women of color. She is a co-editor of the groundbreaking book This Bridge Called My Back: Writings by Radical Women of Color, and playright of the production New Fire: To Make Things Right Again.

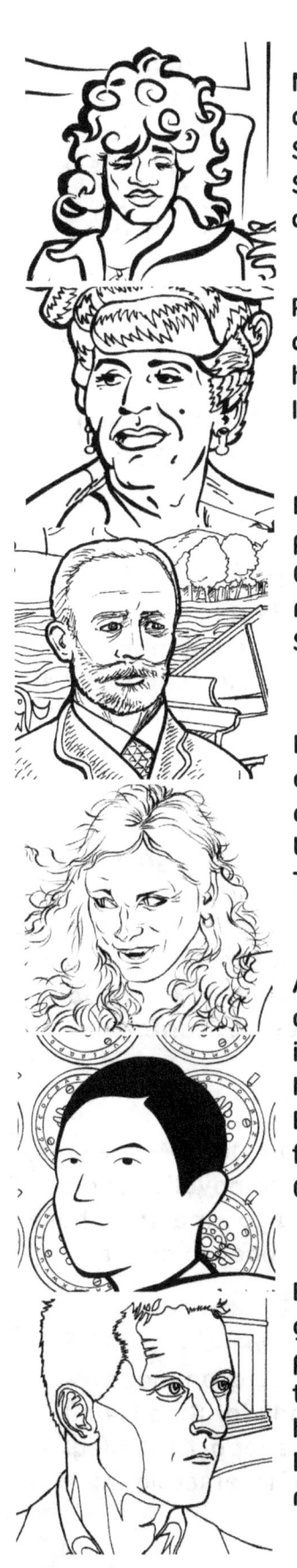

Marsha P. Johnson was one of the first trans women to fight back at the police during the Stonewall riots. Johnson founded the Street Transvestite Action Revolutionaries (STAR) with her friend Sylvia Rivera, bringing food and clothing to homeless trans, drag queen and other street youth.

Paul Lynde was a noted character actor with a distinctively campy and snarky persona that often poked fun at his barely-in-the-closet homosexuality. Dom DeLuise was an American actor and comedian. it Is not known if he was gay or bi, but, I mean, really.

Discussion of Tchaikovsky's personal life, especially his sexuality, has perhaps been the most extensive of any composer in the 19th century. Considerable confusion has come from Soviet efforts to expunge all references to same-sex attraction, portraying him as a heterosexual. Still, biographers have generally agreed that Tchaikovsky was gay.

Laura Jane Grace is the founder, lead singer, guitarist, and songwriter of the punk rock band Against Me!. In 2012, Laura publicly came out as a transgender woman. She has since been involved in efforts to benefit the trans community. In 2014, the band's 6th studio album, Transgender Dysphoria Blues, was released.

Alan Turing is widely considered to be the father of theoretical computer science and artificial intelligence, playing a pivotal role in cracking coded messages that enabled the Allies to defeat the Nazis. It has been estimated that his work shortened the war in Europe by as many as four years. Turing was prosecuted in 1952 for homosexual acts, when such behavior was still a criminal act. Queen Elizabeth II granted him a posthumous pardon in 2013.

Born to a prominent Austrian industrial family, Ludwig Wittgenstein gave up a promising engineering career to focus on work in the philosophy of logic and language. With his two best known works, the Tractatus Logico-Philosophicus and Philosophical Investigations, he twice revolutionized the study of language. Never married, he was known to have loving relationships with both men and women, most notably with David Pinsent during their years together at Cambridge.

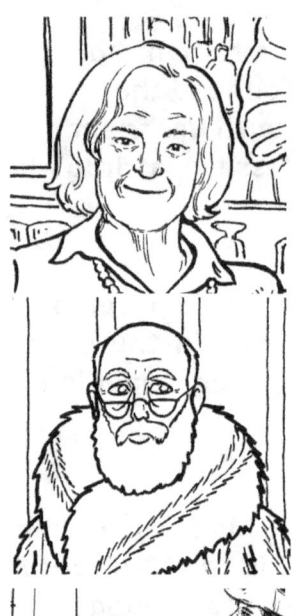

Charlotte von Mahlsdorf was born the child of a Nazi. When her father planned to shoot his pacifist 'son', she killed him with a rolling pin. Later she worked as a second-hand goods dealer and dressed in a more feminine way. The Grunderzeit Museum (a museum of every-day items), of which Charlotte was founder, displays the now historical household items she had scavenged and saved from bombed-out homes.

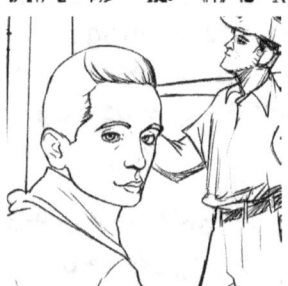

"I'm neither one thing nor the other particularly. I am fortunate in that I am apparently reasonably undersexed or something ... I've never said that I was gay and I've never said that I wasn't ... what I'm trying to say is that I am a person before I am anything else."
-Edward Gorey

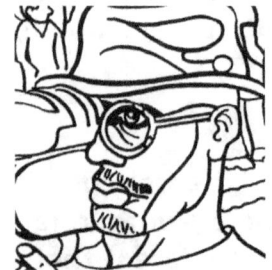

JC Leyendecker was one of the preeminent American illustrators of the early 20th century. He is best known for his trade character, The Arrow Collar Man. Leyendecker excelled at depicting male homosocial spaces (locker rooms, clubhouses, tailoring shops) and extraordinarily handsome young men. This could possibly be due to Leyendecker being gay.

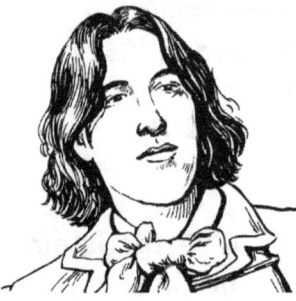

Marlon Riggs was a filmmaker, educator, poet, and gay rights activist. He produced, wrote, and directed several television documentaries, including Ethnic Notions, Tongues Untied, Color Adjustment, and Black is... Black Ain't. Riggs' aesthetically innovative and socially provoca-tive films examine past and present representations of race and sexuality in America. His Collection is now housed at Stanford University Libraries.

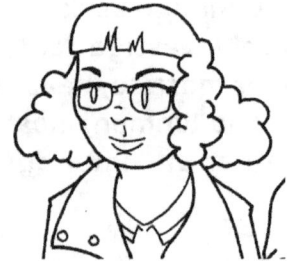

At the height of his popularity in Victorian London, Oscar Wilde was considered the greatest Irish poet, playwright, and novelist of his time. After his arrest and conviction he became a gay martyr whose greatest authorship, remains what we consider, modern queer identity.

G.L.O.S.S. is a punk rock band from Olympia, Washington made up exclusively of trans women. Their name stands for Girls Living Outside of Society's Shit. Their lyrics detail and support the idea of trans liberation in culture through the lens of intersectional feminism and a healthy dose of anarchy.

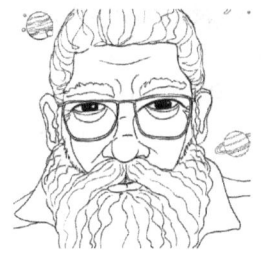

Samuel Delany is an American author, professor, and literary critic. His work includes, queer-inclusive science fiction classics such as Babel-17, Dhalgren, Equinox, Stars In My Pocket Like Grains of Sand, The Einstein Intersection and Triton. He's also really cool.

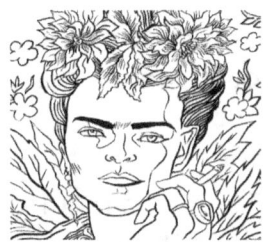

Frida Kahlo was a Mexican painter known for her self-portraits. The bisexual Kahlo had many affairs, including with Isamu Noguchi and Josephine Baker. It was not until the end of the 1970s, with the beginning of Neomexicanismo, that she became well-known to the public.

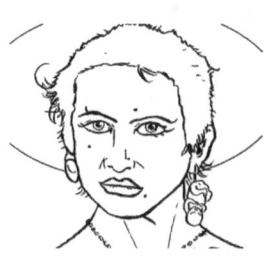

In the late 1980s, Jerome Caja became a well-known artistic personality within the radical gay scene of San Francisco. He performed as a drag queen, Queercore performance artist, and go-go dancer in the city's queer punk nightclubs, going on to craft miniature, mixed-media artwork using everyday materials (particularly those used by drag queens, including nail polish, sequins, lace, glitter, etc.). Caja died of AIDS in 1995, his memorial service held in SF's Hole in the Wall bar. He gifted his unsold art-work to the SFMOMA. Far from forgotten, Caja's personal papers and effects are now archived in the Smithsonian Institution.

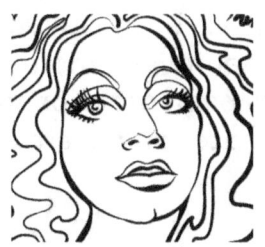

Holly Woodlawn was a transgender Puerto Rican actress and Warhol superstar who appeared in his movies Trash, and Women in Revolt. She was probably best known as the "he who was a she" in Lou Reed's hit pop song "Walk on the Wild Side". And she was purdy.

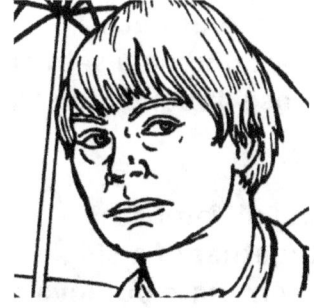

The enfant terrible of British letters in the 1950's, philosopher and novelist Iris Murdoch gained as much notoriety for her romances with both men and women as for her witty novels of ideas. Her philosophical writings placed love at the center of ethics. Her marriage to literary critic John Bayley lasted from 1956 to her death from Alzheimer's disease in 1999.

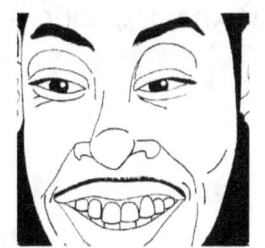

Kortney Ryan Ziegler is an African American filmmaker, scholar, and tech innovator. His award-winning documentary, Still Black, was one of the first to provide an in-depth portrait of the lives of Black trans men. In 2013, he founded Trans*H4CK an incubator for the creation of apps that serve the needs and interests of the trans* community. Ziegler holds a PhD in African American Studies from Northwestern University, where he was the first graduate to receive this degree.

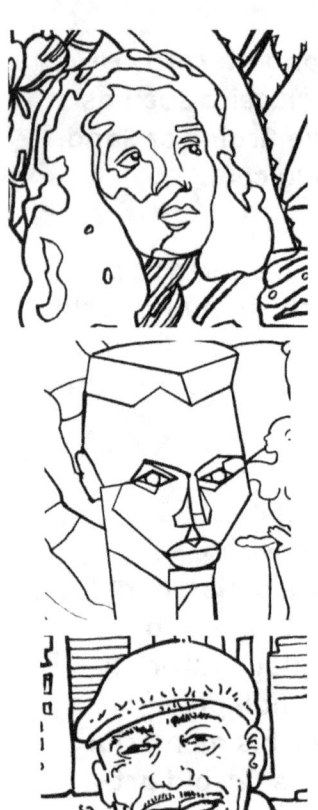

Chavela Vargas was a Costa-Rican born Mexican singer who wildly embraced her queerness in public during a time when it was not culturally acceptable; however, the public adored her for it. With her rough tenderness, she influenced several artists including the painter Frida Kahlo (a former lover) and director Pedro Almodovar.

"I go feminine, I go masculine. I am both, actually. I think the male side is a bit stronger in me, and I have to tone it down sometimes. I'm not like a normal woman, that's for sure." -Grace Jones

Kylar Broadus is a former law professor (and the first trans faculty member ever) at Lincoln University in Missouri. He was the first trans person to testify before the US Senate last year, in support of the Employment Non-Discrimation Act. Founder of the Trans People of Color Coalition in 2010 he was also appointed to the Rules Committee for the 2012 Democratic National Convention.

Growing up, we all need heroes, people who do the things we need done, but can't always do for ourselves. For people in the LGBTQUAI community who are from their youngest days ostracized, misunderstood, and subject to threat of violence by both their peers and those in positions of authority, knowing that there have been other people in this world who have faced the same odds or greater and overcome is an indispensable source of inspiration.

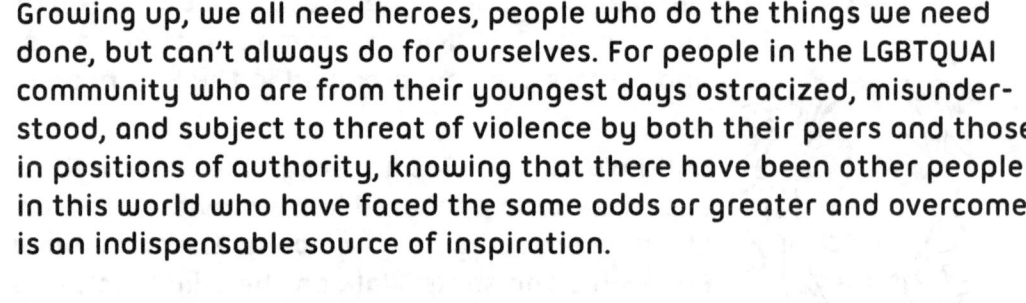

Among us there are figures from our history without whom we could not enjoy the openness and liberty we have today, and as each generation of queer folk emerges with new identities and new sets of problems, new heroes provide inspiration and a sense of belonging to those facing their own struggles.

The Queer Heroes Coloring Book is designed to bring different orientations, gender identities, and generations together in a single volume so that all of us, queer and straight alike, can share our love of some special people in history, politics, science, and the arts who have shown us the way forward.

Thank you and happy coloring,

Tara Madison Avery

www.ingramcontent.com/pod-product-compliance
Lightning Source LLC
Chambersburg PA
CBHW080848170526
45158CB00009B/2667